UNSTUCK

How to Stop Reacting, Start Responding, and Create Lasting Inner Peace

DANIEL SUNDAHL

For more information, email daniel@dansunhealth.com

ISBN: 979-8-90057-287-1 - Ebook
ISBN: 979-8-90057-288-8 - Paperback
ISBN: 979-8-90057-289-5 - Hardcover

To all of you who helped me when I needed support the most.

You know who you are…

Thank You

CONTENTS

INTRODUCTION

THINK OF THE last time you felt truly derailed. Maybe it was the sudden heat of an argument with your partner or the icy disappointment when a friend betrayed your trust. Perhaps it was simply a stranger whose actions challenged your belief in how a civilized community should be. In that moment of shock, frustration, or anger, how did your body and mind react? Did your heart rate increase? Did you feel a tightness in your chest, a knot in your stomach, or a lump in your throat? Did you get defensive and immediately try to convince the other person they were wrong? Or did it just stick with you for a long time and you couldn't shake it?

These moments of conflict are symptoms of a deeper phenomenon. We all live within a carefully constructed bubble of deeply held beliefs about how we think the world *should* be. It's our program that defines our versions of fairness, respect, and success. When your family, friends, or even the general public enter your bubble with a program that doesn't align with yours, conflict and deep frustration can be the result.

The solution is in understanding how and why you react to conflict, not escaping it. It's about learning to identify, define, and live by what really matters to you, realizing that others can do the same without pushing your buttons. Let others live within their beliefs and their own bubbles, and limit their authority in determining how you should feel. This book will reveal what drives you and why you react the way you do to others' actions. When you know this, you're less likely to react blindly and instead respond with intention. You will discover the definitive roadmap for that self-discovery that I call The Emotional Diagnostic Tool. This approach allows you to reverse-engineer negative feelings, build self-efficacy by confirming your personal values, and buffer yourself from the world's chaos. This happens when you avoid relying on others to validate what matters to you and start advocating for yourself.

My expertise in the human stress response has been validated by decades of intensive, real-world application with two decades of personal experience. I operated in the most high-stakes environments life can offer, working full-time as an Advanced Care Paramedic and Firefighter in a busy, metro service. I then pursued rigorous education to become a Registered Counseling Therapist specializing in trauma, relationships, and addiction. I have seen, firsthand, what happens when people live in misalignment, the burnout, the broken relationships, and the lasting trauma it can cause. Crucially, I have also witnessed the profound healing and post-traumatic growth that occurs when an individual finds their true path and lives in alignment with who they actually are at their core. The methods outlined in this book have dramatically changed my life and the lives of the people I work with.

By engaging with the exercises and principles in this book, you will learn to navigate inevitable "core belief bubble collisions" with others and move forward with tranquility and clarity. You will gain the ability to set boundaries that feel authentic, make decisions that align with your integrity, and finally quiet the internal noise that comes from living a life dictated by external expectations and gratification.

Eventually, situations that caused past conflicts won't affect you as deeply; you will become abundantly self-empowered and even empathize with those trying to derail you.

The principles outlined here are the same tools I use every day to help my clients move past paralyzing trauma, depression, anxiety, and relationship conflict. When you learn to define your values, your relationships improve, your professional life stabilizes, and your stress response is not as intense. This process works.

This book can give you more than just personal peace. By understanding your own values and learning to self-validate them, you can gain a pluralistic mindset, which means you get the ability to see several perspectives at the same time along with the profound empathy needed to understand why others respond and react the way they do, while limiting expectations of their behaviour. The more grounded you become, the more powerfully you can contribute to your family, your community, and the world. Giving unconditionally, lowering the stress of expectations, and becoming abundant and self-empowered are the rewards this book offers.

It is important to understand that the goal of this book is not to deny your pain or to stop you from ever feeling "bad" again. Negative emotions are natural and are vital signals from your nervous system telling you that something important requires your attention. In most circumstances, feeling anger, grief, or fear is a normative response to life's challenges. Instead, the goal is learning how to listen to these signals without being overwhelmed by them, and regulate them in positive ways so you can remain in the driver's seat of your life.

Don't mistake the discomfort of today for a temporary problem. The internal friction you feel, the constant struggle, the lingering resentment will only grow the longer you ignore the misalignment. Waiting to find your true path is delaying your peace.

The collision has already begun. Are you ready to stop reacting and start leading and living in alignment with your true self? Turn the page and begin the journey to become *Unstuck* and unleash inner peace through your own unshakable conviction.

A NOTE BEFORE WE BEGIN

I WANT TO be completely honest with you: growth is rarely a comfortable process. In the chapters ahead, I'm going to ask you to look closely at your values, your reactions, and perhaps some of the uncomfortable challenges that have left you feeling depleted or stuck. When we go deep into the mechanics of your inner peace, you might find that certain topics feel a bit heavy or "activating."

I want you to know right now that it is perfectly okay, and even healthy, to put this book down if you start to feel overwhelmed. As a therapist and a former first responder, I've learned that pushing through significant distress when you're not ready for it rarely leads to genuine healing. This isn't a race, and there is no prize for finishing a chapter when your nervous system is telling you to pause. If you feel your pulse quicken or your mind start to race, take that as a signal to set the book on your nightstand, take a breath, and walk away for as long as you need. This process will be waiting for you whenever you feel ready to engage with it again.

Let's get started.

CHAPTER 1

The Cart, the Judge, and the Power of Self-Validation

MY ENGLISH BULLDOG, Dexter, is not a dog built for distance. He's a low, stocky tank, a 65-pound monument to unconditional love that operates strictly on his own terms. Short bursts of "the zoomies" in the backyard? Absolutely. But try to get him past the driveway for a walk, and he'll plant his rear on the pavement, fix me with a questioning glare, and wait.

Dexter has me well-trained, of course. He knows that if he's going to come with me on my daily 7-kilometre walk, he gets to ride in his dog cart. He greets people and other dogs from the elevated comfort of his moving throne, and I get the added benefit of pushing over 100 pounds of cart and canine for seven kilometers (almost four-and-a-half miles) — excellent exercise for me.

On these treks, it's common for us to encounter owners of more athletic breeds, sleek retrievers and tireless border collies, who will walk past and deliver a swift, silent look of judgment. Sometimes the other dogs jump into the cart with Dexter, gazing up at their owners with an envious expression that clearly says, "Why don't *we* have one of these?" My response is usually a shrug and a smile.

One day, however, the judgment turned verbal. An older man walking a magnificent golden retriever stopped dead in his tracks a few feet ahead of us and zeroed in on Dexter in his cart.

"Why aren't you walking that dog?" he demanded.

I gave my standard reply, calm and factual: "He doesn't walk far, and he overheats easily; it's common with the breed."

The man's judgmental expression hardened. "You should be walking that dog; he could use the exercise." Then, he continued on his way with his athletic, obedient companion.

Yes, he had just *fat-shamed* my bulldog, who is, by the way, at a healthy weight for his breed.

I kept walking, but the interaction lingered like a pebble in my shoe. *How dare he judge me? Who is he to determine what's best for my dog?* His rude comment and judgmental stare clung to me for days. I even stopped walking that particular path with Dexter, fearing a second encounter.

How could a single, 10-second interaction with a stranger profoundly change my behaviour? To figure this out, I decided to "therapize" myself, starting with a common intervention known as Cognitive Behavioural Therapy (CBT). Developed by psychiatrist Aaron Beck in the 1960s, CBT's core principle is simple: Change your thoughts, and you can change your emotions and behaviour (Beck et al. 2024).

Imagine driving a car:

Your thoughts are the steering wheel turning.
Your emotions are the front wheels turning left or right.
The vehicle moving in that direction is your behaviour.
Change your behaviour (car moving) by changing your thoughts (turning the steering wheel).

The goal of traditional CBT is to target and adjust the bad thoughts to improve behaviours associated with conditions like anxiety, depression, and post-traumatic stress disorder (PTSD). But this led me to deeper questions: Why do we turn the steering wheel in the first place? Where do the initial thoughts come from that set our entire mental vehicle in motion? I was letting the man's rudeness change the route of my daily walk. Why did his opinion bother me so much?

This was the perfect opportunity to reverse-engineer my reaction using my Emotional Diagnostic Tool (EDT). This tool shifts the focus from mindless reacting to thoughtful responding. Here is how I applied the 4 steps of the EDT to the man on the path (we will dive into each step in detail later in the book):

Step 1: Recognize the Upset: I acknowledged that I was upset and that my behaviour had changed (by avoiding the path). I asked myself what I was feeling; was I feeling it anywhere in my body? When I was away from the man, my jaw was clenched, and I hadn't noticed it. And I knew I felt it in my mind: I was mad, agitated, and if I'm being honest, a bit insecure.

Step 2: Identify the Challenged Core Value: The interaction directly challenged my values of Respect and Kindness. I have my top 10 core values as the backdrop of my phone so I can easily access them.

Step 3: Determine the Source of the Challenge: I asked, "Is my value being challenged by what I did or by what someone *else* did?" Clearly, it was challenged by the man's rude behaviour.

Step 4: Self-Validate the Core Value: This is the most critical step. I reminded myself that I have the power to validate my own values, not others. I stated my predetermined action statements:

I validate my core value of Respect by respecting myself and respecting others.

I validate my core value of Kindness by being kind to others.

I then use my sovereignty (self-empowering) statement: *My core values of Respect and Kindness have been challenged but are intact and self-validated. I was kind and respectful in the interaction. The rude man can do and think as he wishes without challenging my character or changing my behaviour.*

I instantly felt better and was no longer emotionally challenged by this stranger. But something more profound happened when I confirmed that my values were internally validated and intact, I moved beyond reactivity and into empathy. My thoughts shifted from *How dare he?* to *What happened to this man that made him feel it was okay to judge me?* I began to realize that his behaviour and response to Dexter and me had very little to do with me or how I treated my dog.

The real-world result was that my behaviour changed again. Instead of avoiding the pathway, I returned to it. The fear was replaced by curiosity; I even hoped to see him again, just to ask what bothered him so much about me and Dexter's cart. Though I never saw him again, I was curious to learn of his experiences prior to our meeting. By reverse-engineering my reaction, using the Emotional Diagnostic Tool, I was able to shift my perspective, which changed my thoughts, and led to a complete behavioural change. Here's the complete Emotional Diagnostic Tool overview that you can reference as you make your way through this book:

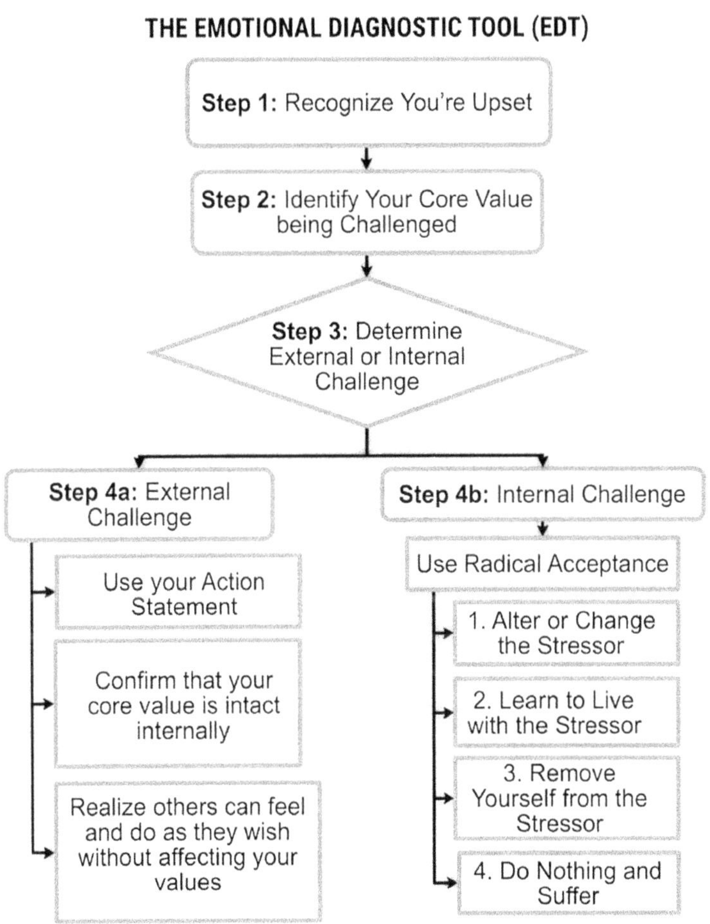

There are, of course, nuances to this, and we'll explore them in later chapters. First, let's explore the very foundation of this entire process: What makes you think the way you do, and how does your bubble of core beliefs develop?

CHAPTER 2

How Belief Systems are Built

"We are what we are because we have been what we have been, and what is needed for solving the problems of human life and motives is not moral estimates but more knowledge."

– Sigmund Freud

SINCE THE AGE of seven, your mind has been primarily functioning in a theta brainwave state, effectively operating like a hypnotic recording device. According to Bruce H. Lipton, Ph.D (2005), author of *The Biology of Belief*, this data, collected during the first seven years of your life, accounts for 95 percent of your daily behaviour as an adult.

The bulk of your fundamental understanding of the world, rules of love, definitions of safety, and limits of possibility was burrowed straight into your subconscious without critical review. Before you could think critically, you were recording the universe as you experienced it. Your adult reality was set by the time you were in second grade, and you didn't even remember making the recording.

This chapter is about tracing that recording: exploring how the raw data of your childhood experience gets converted into the foundation of your adult core beliefs, drawing on the groundbreaking research of cellular biologist Bruce H. Lipton, the compelling psychological evidence presented in David Robson's book *The Expectation Effect: How Your Mindset Can Transform Your Life* (2022), and the neurobiologist and organizational psychologist Nicole Vignola. Understanding how your belief system is created is the first step toward consciously rewiring the self-limiting programming that may be dictating your life.

Nicole Vignola (2024), in her book *Rewire: Break the Cycle, Alter Your Thoughts and Create Lasting Change,* explains how core beliefs form in childhood through the lens of an ever-changing brain and repetitive exposure. Her model essentially presents the brain as a dynamic system that is subconsciously "programmed" by its early environment. To understand how your belief system developed, you must first understand the operating system of your young brain. Your brain's electrical activity is measured in cycles per second (Hertz) and shifts dramatically as you mature. These brainwave states determine how your mind processes information (Lipton 2005):

Age Range	Primary Brainwave State	Function	Information Processing
Birth–2 Years	**Delta** **(0.5–4 Hz)**	Sleep, Unconscious	Primarily for survival programming and physical growth.
2–6 Years	**Theta (4–8 Hz)**	Hypnagogic, Dreamlike	Hypnotic recording. Ideal for imaginative play and deep subconscious learning.

6–12 Years	**Alpha (8–12 Hz)**	Calm, Reflective	Onset of conscious thought and logical reasoning. Transition from learning to reasoning.
12+ Years	**Beta (12–30 Hz)**	Alert, Conscious	Active thinking, decision-making, and critical assessment.

As Bruce H. Lipton, Ph.D. (2005) details in his work, the dominant theta state is key. Lipton argues that during this period, you were highly suggestible, directly absorbing the surrounding environment, verbal cues, the emotional climate, and your parents' responses as irrefutable truths. You didn't yet have the thinking capacity (the beta state) to compare, contrast, or critically evaluate the information being downloaded.

Imagine a computer receiving an operating system (OS). If you install the OS without a firewall or antivirus, every piece of data is accepted as legitimate. That is your mind as a child. It is an open gate, uncritically downloading your parental and cultural programs, which will then run your life as an adult. Lipton asserts that these programs, stored in your subconscious, account for 95 percent of your daily behaviour as an adult (2005). This means that the vast majority of your choices, reactions, and emotional responses are determined by programs you didn't consciously choose.

The content of your childhood hypnotic recording falls into three primary categories:

1. **Models of Self-Worth and Identity**

   Observation: You see how your parents respond to your mistakes (e.g., a spilled drink).

   If your parent responds with frustration and anger ("You are so careless!"), you record the belief: *"I am fundamentally flawed" or "Mistakes mean punishment."*

   Potential Core Belief Result if repeated often: "I am not good enough" or **"My worth is conditional."**

2. **Models of Relationships and Love**

   Observation: You observe how your caregivers/parents interact with each other (e.g., affection, conflict, or silence). If affection is only shown after an achievement or gift, you record: *Love is transactional and must be earned.*

   Potential Core Belief Result: "I must please others to be loved" or **"Trust is dangerous."**

3. **Models of Possibility and Abundance**

   Observation: You constantly hear about financial stress or scarcity ("We can't afford that," "Money is the root of all evil"). Your subconscious records the association: *The world is a place of lack and struggle.*

   Potential Core Belief Result: "Life is hard" or **"Success requires immense, painful sacrifice."**

These deeply ingrained childhood experiences and observations shape the subconscious beliefs that dictate your default responses and self-perception well into adulthood (Vignola 2024). Vignola emphasizes that many people unknowingly live a life programmed by their early environments, which is why so much conscious effort is needed later to "upgrade the software" to *rewire* those limiting beliefs. These programs, cemented during the theta phase in your childhood, are what we call core beliefs. They are the deeply held, often unconscious, fundamental assumptions that you use to interpret every new experience in your life. As you matured and the dominant brainwave state shifted to alpha and beta, you gained the capacity for conscious, critical thought. However, you didn't change the core beliefs; you simply started filtering your life experiences *through* them.

Once your core belief is established, your subconscious goes to great lengths to preserve it. This is due to a powerful psychological phenomenon known as *confirmation bias*. Research by Raymond Nickerson, PhD, tells us that confirmation bias is the tendency to search for, interpret, favour, and recall information in ways that confirm or support your prior beliefs or values (1998). Even if those beliefs make you feel bad.

How Confirmation Bias Works:

Scenario: You have the core belief "I am not good enough," and you are applying for a new job. Your subconscious filter is actively seeking evidence to confirm your core belief that you are not good enough.

If Rejected: "See? I knew it. I am not good enough for that." Your belief is confirmed and strengthened.

If Accepted: Your subconscious may dismiss the evidence: "It was luck," or "They hired you because they need someone desperately." The positive data is rejected, and your core belief remains untouched.

This self-fulfilling loop ensures that the information recorded during the first seven years of your life remains active, often overriding conscious logic and willpower. Your beliefs are so deeply embedded that your adult brain sees them not as *opinions* but as *facts* about your reality. Of course, not all of your core beliefs are bad. A healthy upbringing can lead to many positive and helpful core beliefs, and most of us have a blend of positive and negative programming. The focus of this book is to counter your core beliefs that have become *maladaptive* (inadequate adaptation). It really *is* all about your childhood.

The connection between your internalized core beliefs and your lived experience is not merely theoretical; it is measurable and physiological. David Robson's book, *The Expectation Effect* meticulously documents how your expectations, which are conscious reflections of your subconscious core beliefs, physically alter your body and environments (2022). Robson highlights the power of mindset, which we'll define as the beliefs you hold about a given domain (e.g., aging, stress, food). If you have the core belief "Stress is dangerous and debilitating," your body will respond dramatically differently to a stressful situation than someone who holds the belief "Stress is energizing and aids performance." Robson presents various examples that illustrate the profound mind-body connection, where your subconscious beliefs about effort, food, and health literally become your physical reality.

Perhaps the most astonishing demonstration of the expectation effect comes from a study involving hotel chambermaids (Crum and Langer 2007). This group performs extremely strenuous physical labour by cleaning rooms, changing linens, and pushing heavy carts, yet, when surveyed, most reported not getting enough exercise and saw their work as merely a *job*, not a workout. Their core belief was: *"I am sedentary and unhealthy."*

Psychologists divided 84 chambermaids across seven hotels into two groups:

1. **The Informed Group:** This group received detailed information and posters explaining that their daily work, vacuuming for 15 minutes, pushing the cart for 30 minutes, and scrubbing for 10 minutes, easily met and often exceeded the Surgeon General's daily recommendation for an active lifestyle. Their work was reframed as a valuable form of exercise.
2. **The Control Group:** This group received no information. They continued their work as usual.

Neither group changed their behaviour or workload. Their only difference was the belief about their activity. The results, measured after just four weeks, were remarkable. The Informed Group showed significant physiological improvements: a drop in body weight, reductions in body fat and Body Mass Index (BMI), and a significant 10-point drop in systolic blood pressure. This group also reported that their habits had not changed over the 30-day study period with respect to either decreased caloric intake or increased exercise. The Control Group, performing the exact same labour, showed no such improvements. The physical benefits of the labour were only unlocked when the mind adopted the belief (the expectation) that it was receiving exercise.

This study reveals that your body is constantly taking cues from your childhood programming, not just from your current experiences. If your core belief about work, effort, or even age is that it is *draining* and *unhealthy*, your body will manifest that belief. Conversely, if you reprogram that core belief, your body can deliver tangible, measurable health benefits, regardless of your perceived reality, meaning: Your subconscious believes its own operating system over the reality of your external experiences.

Robson presents several other examples across various domains that illustrate the profound mind-body connection. A classic example is the placebo effect, in which an inert substance (such as a sugar pill) delivers therapeutic benefits because the patient *believes* it will. This is a direct manifestation of a positive expectation. On the other hand, the nocebo effect shows that negative expectations and core beliefs about vulnerability or inevitable failure can actively induce adverse health outcomes, side effects, or increased pain (Häuser et al. 2012). If you believe your life is always difficult (a core belief), the nocebo effect may manifest physically as chronic pain or exhaustion to prove your belief to be true. Which belief do you tend to identify with: I'm a survivor, or I'm a victim?

As a firefighter, I always had difficulties with knots. I just couldn't wrap my head around them and wished we could just use carabiners to attach equipment and ropes together. I now know that I was bad at knots because I believed I was bad at knots. When I was first learning to interpret 12-lead electrocardiograms (ECGs), the electrical activity of the human heart, I also found it difficult to understand. But in this case, I told myself I would be the best 12-lead interpreter in our class. I believed it, studied it, and realized that goal by maintaining that mindset all throughout my career.

If you believe you're not good at baking — or anything else — then you won't be. If you believe you're great at it, then you'll more likely be good at it.

In my experience with emergency services, we always have that one person we call a black cloud. It means that when they are on shift, they will get all the crazy calls. They know it, and everyone who works with them knows it. There are white cloud people as well, firefighters who have never been on a structure fire while everyone else in the department has, or paramedics who have never had to resuscitate anyone. I believe this is their core belief manifesting into reality. Manifesting your reality by changing your beliefs may sound unbelievable and floofy to you, but I see it happen to others all the time.

It's the basis of Rhonda Byrne's book *The Secret* (2006). In her book, Rhonda Byrne argues that our thoughts have the power to attract the life we want. While there is power in a positive mindset, the "mental abundance" I will describe in this book goes a step further. It isn't just about *thinking* your way to a better life; it's about *living* your way to a more profound peace by aligning every action with your core values. A positive mindset is about what you can get from the world; mental abundance is about who you become within it.

Try this little experiment. Just before you fall asleep tonight, tell yourself, *"Something extraordinary is going to happen to me tomorrow."* Repeat it to yourself three times, then go to sleep. You may be surprised by what the next day brings.

Research has shown that mere beliefs about the nature of stress are more critical than the stress itself (Crum et al. 2013). Individuals who view stress as debilitating show an increased risk of health issues, like cardiovascular strain, because their mindset triggers an unhealthy release of cortisol and constricts blood vessels. Individuals who are taught to view stress responses (like a racing heart) as the body preparing for action show healthier physiological responses, such as regulated cortisol levels and more open blood vessels.

Your core belief about stress, learned from observing how your parents handled pressure, literally determines whether stress harms or helps you. The most potent way beliefs manifest into your reality is through the self-fulfilling prophecy, which links the core belief, the behavioural action, and the external outcome:

Core Belief (Subconscious): "I am destined to fail at money."

Expectation (Conscious): *I will probably lose this investment.* (The Expectation Effect is engaged).

Behaviour (Lipton's 95 percent): You subconsciously avoid learning new financial literacy skills, engage in self-sabotaging investment risks, or avoid taking necessary career leaps.

Outcome: The investment is lost or the career stagnates.

Confirmation: "See? I knew I was destined to fail at money." The core belief is confirmed and reinforced.

My self-fulfilling prophecy about knots was that I couldn't make sense of how the rope twisted on itself, so I failed even before I tried. When I did inevitably fail, I confirmed to myself that I was bad at knots.

This cycle demonstrates the terrifying efficiency of your subconscious mind. It does not judge your belief; it simply ensures that the programs it runs from your childhood are always validated by the outside world. Your brain is a survival organ that adapts to keep its function as efficient as possible above all else, it's priority isn't to make you happy. The realization that your life is primarily run by programs instilled before you were seven can be discouraging. However, understanding this programming is fundamentally empowering, for it means that the limitations you face are not inherent truths of the universe; they are simply learned programs that can be edited.

Traditional talk therapy operates primarily in the conscious mind (the beta state). While identifying a maladaptive core belief, such as "I think I'm not worthy of love" is a necessary first step in the rewiring process, simply *knowing* the belief does not remove the hypnotic childhood belief from your subconscious. Think of it like trying to change a computer program by yelling at the monitor. The input must be included in the programming code itself. This is where the work shifts from *realization* (CBT's focus on the thought) to *reprogramming* (our focus in this book and on your core values). It's changing why we think what we believe before we even turn the steering wheel in the CBT vehicle.

Lipton's work emphasizes that since the subconscious mind was programmed during a relaxed, highly receptive state (theta), the most effective way to reprogram it as an adult is to return to similar states:

Habit Repetition: Your subconscious learns by habit. Consistently practicing a new positive behaviour (even if it feels inauthentic) will eventually override your old program and become your new normal.

Energy Psychology (e.g., Theta Healing, Hypnosis): Accessing your subconscious during the theta state, such as through deep meditation or hypnosis, allows you to bypass your critical, conscious mind and instill new beliefs directly (Kirsch 2011).

Psychedelic Therapies (Ketamine for Trauma): Ketamine puts the brain into a delta/theta wave state, allowing for increased connectivity in your brain (Ní Dhúill et al. 2019). This helps build new programs with less resistance.

The Emotional Diagnostic Tool - EDT (The Focus of This Book): This method is a form of *conscious, immediate belief validation* that uses your core value system to rapidly dismantle your confirmation bias cycle and create new, helpful core beliefs about yourself.

The EDT works by inserting a conscious, validated self-affirmation into your reactive moment, preventing your negative core belief from running its automated programming.

When the man judged my dog-walking choice, my immediate reaction was run by the old, theta-programmed script: *I have been criticized, therefore I am flawed, therefore I must retreat.* By using the EDT, I consciously inserted my self-validated values: *My value of respect is intact because **I** was respectful. His judgment is irrelevant to **my** truth.* This immediate, self-validating thought short-circuited my automatic negative thought, preventing the core belief of "I am not good enough" from being reinforced by the man's rude comment.

The study of belief system development places the burden of responsibility squarely on you, not in a punishing way, but in an empowering way. If 95 percent of your life is run by programs you did not consciously choose, then the ultimate act of liberation is to become the conscious programmer of your own mind. You cannot change the observations you recorded as a child, but you *can* change the core beliefs those observations generated. This conscious edit is the key to unlocking your inner peace, overcoming stress, and moving from reactive living (dictated by old programs and the actions of others) to intentional living (guided by self-empowerment).

In the next chapter, you will learn the critical difference between your core beliefs and core values, distinguishing the two components that form your mental operating system. You will explore this system using the analogy of a computer: Core Beliefs are the preinstalled, often flawed, childhood software programs running in the background, while core values are the adult hardware upgrade that you must reconnect with and validate to create a new, powerful operating system for peace and intentional living. We will then fully deconstruct the EDT, providing you with the exact methodology to step into the driver's seat and begin actively rewriting your subconscious programming.

CHAPTER 3

The Internal Operating System: Core Beliefs vs. Core Values

IF CHAPTER 2 established that your childhood experience created the programs that run your life, Chapter 3 is about understanding the difference between those automatic, often problematic programs and the foundation that is your system of core values. Your mind functions like a complex computer operating system (OS).

When you were 0–7 years old, the OS was installed with a set of default settings and preloaded applications; these are your core beliefs. Remember, your brain isn't designed to keep you happy; it's a survival organ, so it will record everything, your good (I am loved) and bad (I am not lovable) core beliefs. Beneath that *software* layer lies the *hardware* itself: the central processing unit (CPU), the fundamental parts that dictate how you perceive your world and respond. That hardware represents your core values.

The goal of this chapter is to define these two components, demonstrate how they interact in your life, and reveal why aligning your life with your core values is a path to stress resilience, emotional stability, and self-empowerment. This book is about *you* taking complete control of your core values, your hardware, and programming them to your advantage. This is a complete rewiring upgrade for your mind.

In your mental operating system, the distinction between beliefs and values is crucial. One is a potentially corrupted, maladaptive program (core beliefs), and the other is a truth about who you are now and how you react and connect with others (core values). *Maladaptive* describes a behaviour, thought, or reaction that helps you get through the next five minutes but hurts you over the next five years. Simply put, it is a "short-term fix with a long-term cost." When you're under pressure, your brain wants relief at *that* instant. Maladaptive choices are the shortcuts your brain takes to numb pain, avoid conflict, or feel in control, even if those choices eventually make your life harder. Maladaptive core beliefs are the deeply ingrained, often subconscious assumptions about yourself, the world, and your relationship to it. They are the learned interpretations of reality that are ingrained during the highly suggestive theta brainwave state of your childhood.

Maladaptive Core Beliefs

Core Belief Type	Description	Examples
Helplessness/ Uncontrollability	The belief that you are unable to influence outcomes or protect yourself from harm	"I am incapable of succeeding on my own."
Unlovability/ Unworthiness	The belief about your personal defectiveness and that you are flawed.	"Nobody can love the real me; I'm a bad person."

Danger/Threat	The belief that the world is hostile and unsafe	"The world is dangerous; disaster is always imminent."

Core beliefs can be limiting or empowering, but are *always* conditional because they were based on a specific set of circumstances (your childhood environment). They are the assumptions that run your day-to-day automatic behaviours as an adult, the 95 percent Lipton speaks of. Core beliefs are not all bad, but the focus of this book is to reverse-engineer problematic emotions and behaviours, leaving the good bits untouched, if not improved.

Core values, on the other hand, are the fundamental standards, ideals, and principles that determine what is important to you now, not as a child, and how you wish to conduct your life as a wise, independent adult. They are the traits, qualities, and behaviours that you consider essential to your true adult self and your personal integrity.

Core Values

Characteristic	Description	Examples
Source	Internal choice, intrinsic motivation, and reflection on integrity	Kindness, Integrity, Growth, Freedom, Loyalty, Respect
Nature	Prescriptive, self-validating, relatively fixed (though they can be prioritized)	Prescribing *how* you choose to act and live

Impact	Guide ethical choice, provide inner validation, and ensure inner peace	Determine the process of a decision Responding instead of reacting Self-Empowerment

While your core belief might be "I must please everyone to be accepted," your corresponding core value might be being true to who you are (Authenticity). Your core belief is the issue; your core value is how we can change it through repetition and the development of new automatic ways of thinking. The moment a stressor arises, these two components may conflict, creating a sense of misalignment.

Let's return to the man fat-shaming Dexter: The man's rude comment challenges my dog-walking choice, which triggers my core belief: "I am flawed/bad." The results are emotions of shame, anger, and fear, and the behaviours are avoidance and withdrawal from the path. The resulting behaviour clashes with my inherent desire to live by my core values of Respect, Kindness, and Vitality. My emotional discomfort lingers for days because the *action* (retreating due to fear of judgment) did not align with my *values* (acting with respectful confidence). Recognizing that the man's rude comment challenged my values of respect and kindness is an essential component of The Emotional Diagnostic Tool (EDT), to be discussed in more detail later.

When your core belief (child) and core value (adult) clash, the lingering distress is your internal OS crashing. It's the feeling you have of being misaligned, a round peg trying to fit in a square hole, the feeling of swimming upstream. Your self-worth is being challenged by an outdated, fear-based program initiated by something beyond your control (like the man's rude comment). If your core values are the template for decision-making, validation, and resilience, then actively identifying and defining them is the most critical step in becoming *unstuck*.

You make thousands of decisions daily, mostly subconsciously. When faced with a significant choice, career change, difficult conversation, or confrontation, core values serve as a decision-making tool to help align who you are with the decisions you make.

- Scenario: You are offered a high-paying job that requires you to work 80 hours a week and travel constantly.
    - Without consulting your values, you might be guided by your core belief, "Success requires money," and take the job, leading to burnout.
    - Consulting Values: If your top core values are Family and Balance, your compass immediately tells you the new job is steering you toward a life you don't actually want, regardless of the pay. You can then consciously choose the path that aligns with your self-validated truth — your core values — the round peg fitting into the round hole, swimming with the current, living in alignment with your true self.

As introduced in the first chapter, self-validation is the key to decoupling your self-worth from external opinions. When you know your core values, you shift the validation authority from the outside world (other people) to your controllable internal actions. If you let others validate your core value of Kindness, you constantly seek their approval. If they call you unkind, your worth is threatened.

When you self-validate your core values (e.g., "I validate my value of Kindness by speaking to others with empathy, regardless of their reaction"), the judgment of others becomes less relevant. The moment you act in alignment with your stated core value, you are successful, regardless of the outcome or how others respond. Your inner peace is guaranteed because you are the only one with the power to validate your worth. You've become unstuck.

David Robson's work highlights that your mindset determines your physiological responses to stress. When an external crisis hits (a job loss, a critical comment), your values act as an emotional buffer. For example, something happens that triggers your core belief that "I am a failure," and because your subconscious childhood programming believes it, you may begin to feel shame and panic. If you have identified that your values are Perseverance and Growth, the failure is not a statement about your inherent worth (core belief); it is simply an opportunity to enact your core value of Perseverance. The crisis is now a chance to live your highest self, instantly shifting the physiological stress response from debilitating to strengthening.

The principles behind identifying and living by core values are not new. They form the very backbone of Stoic philosophy, a school of thought founded in Athens in the 3rd century BC and championed by figures like Emperor Marcus Aurelius and the former slave Epictetus. The Stoics defined the path to *Eudaimonia* (often translated as flourishing or living well) through alignment with virtue, which is synonymous with core values.

Imagine yourself on your deathbed. What are you thinking about?

As a paramedic, I've been with several people as they died. I'm sure none of them were thinking about the external material items they gained or the self-gratifying events in their lives. It's the most significant perspective shift we will ever face in our lives. How do you live your life? Don't wait for the profound perspective shift of death to judge your life and how you lived it. If you died today, what regrets would you have? Did you live a good life as defined by the Stoics? Living authentically and cultivating deep, meaningful connections with others? Most of the people who died in my presence as an emergency worker didn't know it was going to be their last day. Don't wait to start living in alignment with who you actually are, and use this deathbed mindset to evaluate where you are in your life.

William B. Irvine (2009), author of *A Guide to the Good Life: The ancient art of Stoic Joy,* explains that Stoicism's foundational principle is arguing that wisdom and tranquillity are achieved by focusing solely on one's own judgments and actions while accepting external events.

Within Your Control (Up to You)	**Outside Your Control (Not Up to You)**
Your judgments and opinions	Other people's opinions (the man I met while walking Dexter)
Your impulses and desires	My bulldog Dexter's breed limitations
Your actions and character	The actions and character of others

Epictetus famously summarized this: *"The chief task in life is simply this: to identify and separate matters so that I can say clearly to myself which are externals not under my control, and which have to do with the choices I actually control."*

The Stoics argued that the only things of genuine value are our moral character, our judgment, and our ability to act virtuously. By defining and committing to a core value (e.g., Justice or Courage), you are focusing all your energy on the only thing you can actually control: *your decision to act in alignment with who you truly are.*

The Man's Rude Comment, Reconsidered Through Stoicism

External Challenge (Out of My Control): The man's opinion, his rudeness, his desire to judge me

Internal (In My Control): My choice to respond with Respect and to maintain Kindness, and my judgment to continue my walk with confidence

By applying this philosophy, the man's comment is rendered powerless immediately and instead becomes an opportunity to practice my core values of respect and composure. This is self-validation: winning not by arguing or retreating, but by acting exactly how you wish to be defined in the face of adversity. This deliberate, value-driven action is the source of deep, unshakable inner peace. With this peace, comes the realization that peace doesn't come from an external location, sound, smell, or activity; it's internal and comes from within, no matter where you are. Moving forward, the goal is to make your core values the primary driver and allow them to override the limiting, problematic core beliefs that the old software tries to run. This requires three imperatives:

1: Define Your Core Values

You must rigorously define the core values that make you tick. If one of your values is Growth, determine what action you must take daily to validate it. Your values must be actionable, not aspirational.

Many individuals, organizations, and business models define their core values but fall short of putting them into practice to instill lasting change.

2: Install the Value-Driven Software (Action Statements)

When the old thought of "I must avoid criticism" runs, the new thought, armed with your core value, must immediately interrupt: "I value Courage; therefore, I will proceed with my action, allowing others to have their opinions." **You can't just remove the old programming; it needs to be replaced.**

3: Debug the System in Real Time (The Emotional Diagnostic Tool)

The EDT is the debugging program for your OS. It is a simple process that allows you to pause a negative emotional response, trace it back to the core value being challenged, and instantly self-validate that value, taking the power away from others who have challenged you. Becoming fluent in this diagnostic process ensures that external events can no longer bypass your conscious choice and trigger those maladaptive core belief programs that were installed when you were a child. You are now running on the reliable, resilient foundation of your self-empowered core values. The road to becoming unstuck and unleashing inner peace is, above all else, about guaranteeing that your stress response is always in alignment with your best, highest self, the wise adult version of you. As the new programming takes over, self-empowerment, abundance, and unconditional behaviours become your norm.

Later in this book, I will provide the complete, step-by-step installation guide for your new OS: a detailed breakdown of the EDT that reveals how your core values are stimulated when you experience pleasure and are challenged when you experience discomfort. Knowing this fundamental link allows you to reverse-engineer your feelings, trace a negative emotion back to your challenged value, and consciously shift your behaviour and state of mind.

CHAPTER 4

Fueling Self-Empowerment with Core Values

IMAGINE OWNING A sleek, powerful car that is a representation of your life, that requires fuel or validation to run. For most of us, this car is utterly dependent on external resources: a gas station. Every time you need validation for your worth, your decisions, or your character, you must drive to an external validation station. This is the state of dependence. Every interaction — a promotion, a compliment, a judgmental stare (like the one aimed at Dexter's cart) — is an opportunity to either receive fuel or be denied. Worse, the station attendants (the people who validate or challenge you) often operate on their own schedules and policies. If they choose to deny you fuel, your car stalls, and your core beliefs about scarcity and unworthiness are confirmed.

Now, imagine your car, but with a revolutionary, self-sustaining fuel tank. It generates its own energy based on its internal design. This self-sustaining state, where your worth is validated from within regardless of external circumstances, is the state of *self-empowerment and abundance*, and it is the goal of living by your core values. This chapter will guide you through connecting psychologist

Abraham Maslow's Hierarchy of Needs to your core value system, demonstrating that the Emotional Diagnostic Tool (EDT) is a path to achieving self-actualization and abundance.

In 1943, Maslow introduced his Hierarchy of Needs, a five-stage model of human motivation. Maslow suggested that some lower needs must be met before higher ones can be addressed. Understanding this hierarchy is vital because stress and emotional reactivity often arise when we perceive a threat to our basic needs, triggering our fear-based core beliefs. Abraham Maslow defines *self-actualization*, the tip of his Hierarchy of Needs, as the process of becoming everything you are capable of becoming (1943). It is the point at which you stop living to meet the expectations of others or just to "survive" the day, and start living to fulfill your own unique potential. Maslow famously summed it up by saying: "What a man can be, he must be."

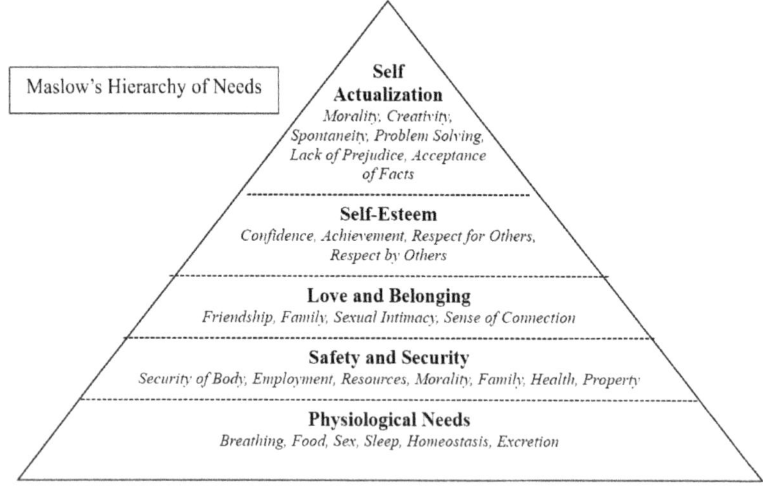

When the lower two tiers are met, you feel stable. When they are threatened, they immediately engage your primal and often maladaptive core beliefs: *The world is unsafe, I must constantly struggle.* The middle tiers address your social and ego needs, and this is where the cycle of external dependence may take hold. You seek connection, often at the cost of your true self. You may confuse belonging with compliance, and adopt others' beliefs and values to secure your acceptance. This is a direct violation of the core value of Authenticity. Esteem needs are seeking prestige and accomplishment. Here, the core belief trap is relying on external measures (titles, money, validation) for self-worth. This makes your self-worth conditional, putting you squarely back at the External Validation Gas Station and keeping you dependent.

At the pinnacle is achieving your full potential, driven by intrinsic growth: self-actualization. In our model, self-actualization leads to the state of Abundance, and the self-filling fuel tank starts to overflow, making you able to offer the abundance to others without condition or reciprocation. It is where you move from needing others to validate your worth to generating your worth from within and offering the overflow (abundance) to others.

The path to Abundance is paved by shifting the source of value validation from the external world to the internal commitment to your core values. The EDT is a method for achieving this shift.

The key characteristic of the abundant, self-empowered person is their unwavering commitment to their core values, even when challenged. The *result* of the action becomes less important than the *action's intention.*

Let's return to the value of Respect (from the Dexter story): If the man judges how I walk my dog and disrespects me, my core belief is triggered, and my sense of self is threatened. I am dependent on his opinion (the gas station). This is a scarcity mindset dependent on others to validate my worth.

If I define my value of Respect as "I treat myself and others with courtesy, regardless of their behaviour," when the man insults my dog and me, I validate my value simply by maintaining my composure. *My self-worth is confirmed by my action, not his reaction,* and my fuel tank is self-filling. This is an abundance mindset resulting from internal validation.

The EDT enables this Abundance Mindset by instantly transforming a perceived external threat (disrespect) into an opportunity to practice a core value (Respect and Empathy).

Author Ryan Holiday (2014), channeling Stoic wisdom, asserts that the challenge we face is not an enemy, but a direct pathway to growth. This view is the beginning of the Abundance Mindset. The *obstacle* (in my example, the man's rude behaviour) is precisely what forces us to use our highest mental faculties to face the challenge and the opportunity to rise above. When an obstacle is viewed through the lens of a core value, it is no longer a setback but a test of Perseverance, Courage, or Integrity. Holiday writes, "The impediment to action advances action. What stands in the way becomes the way."

When you are operating in this state of Abundance, the body and mind respond by viewing the stress as a performance enhancer, thereby supporting your ability to live your values rather than collapse into fear-based core beliefs (Robson 2022). The obstacle is the opportunity to fill your fuel tank.

Maslow differentiated between Deficit Needs (D-Needs) and Being Needs (B-Needs) (Maslow 1968). D-Needs motivate you when you *lack* something. Most of the world operates on D-Needs, constantly trying to fill a hole. The Abundant Life operates entirely on B-Needs or Growth Motivation. Here, the motivation is not to *fill* a deficiency but to *express* your potential and continually realize and live your core values. The self-actualized person seeks out opportunities for Integrity, Growth, and Impact because expressing those values *is* their essential nature. This shift is the definitive move from the External Validation Gas Station to the self-filling tank.

Psychological freedom achieved through self-actualization and empowerment is liberation from external control and dependence on others. For most of our lives, we are unwittingly puppeteered by the external world which control the strings of our emotional state and behaviour.

The Critic (Any Rude Behaviour): Holds the Shame/Anger string. They tug it, and we react by withdrawing or defending.

The Validator (The Boss/Partner): Holds the Joy/Worry string. They offer praise, and we feel joy; they withhold it, and we feel anxiety.

The Past (Core Beliefs): Holds the Avoidance string. An event triggers the old *I am not good enough* belief, and we reactively pull back from new opportunities.

Every time these strings are successfully pulled, your need for validation is confirmed and you remain dependent on the External Validation Station. The EDT is the surgical knife that allows you to consciously cut these strings. By consistently using the steps of the EDT to reverse engineer when you feel bad, you achieve two powerful forms of liberation:

1. Limiting Access to External *Validation*

When you consciously choose to validate your core values of Integrity or Kindness through your own actions, you instantly devalue the need for external praise. The praise becomes pleasant, but not essential, because your self-worth is already confirmed by the internal alignment of being true to who you are. The validator's string loses its tension.

I like the analogy of having a full or empty kitchen. If your kitchen cupboards and fridge are full of pizzas, then when a delivery person comes to your door and offers free pizza, you don't feel a strong need to accept it because you're in a pizza surplus (B-Needs). However, if you have an empty kitchen and are hungry, you'll take the pizza every time, even if it has terrible toppings on it because you're in a pizza deficit (D-Needs).

2. Limiting Access to External *Challenge*

When someone attempts to pull the Anger or Shame string (a challenge), the tool intercedes:

- **Step 1 of EDT (Recognize When Upset):** You feel vulnerable and angry.
- **Step 2 of EDT (Identify Challenged Value):** You realize they are challenging your core value of Respect.
- **Step 3 of EDT (Determine Source):** You confirm they are the source and therefore external.
- **Step 4 of EDT (Validate and Realize Value is Intact):** You conclude: *My value of Respect is validated by my composure, not by their opinion. They can do and think as they wish without challenging who I know I am.*

By refusing to engage the old maladaptive core belief (I am flawed), you render the puppeteer's string useless. The core value acts as a shield. You have successfully limited or removed their access to your emotional center, allowing you to sustain inner peace and control. This is precisely how the Stoics viewed the ultimate freedom, the inner fortress where external events cannot reach you.

The freedom to live your core values, unimpeded by the fear-based demands of core beliefs and external validation, is a path to self-actualization, empowerment, and abundant living. It is the realization that you have the internal resources, the self-filling tank, the full kitchen, to sustain your journey, regardless of the turbulent terrain, the crazy world, or the unreliable gas stations you encounter along the way.

CHAPTER 5

Rewiring the Brain for Peace

HOW, EXACTLY, DOES a conscious choice in a stressful moment, like affirming your value of Integrity after making a mistake, physically override decades of beliefs? The answer lies in the biology of your mind. Your beliefs, your emotions, and your capacity for inner peace are not abstract thoughts; they are rooted in the physical structure of your brain. This chapter will explore the neuroscience of thought, using the analogy of a forest to reveal how you build mental pathways and how the Emotional Diagnostic Tool (EDT) is designed to create new, resilient pathways for abundance and peace.

Your brain contains approximately 86 billion neurons, constantly communicating through electrical and chemical signals. This communication occurs via connections called synapses, which form intricate neural networks. Imagine your brain as a vast, ancient forest. The individual neurons are the trees and roots of the forest. The neural pathways are the paths or trails among the trees. A single thought, memory, or feeling is a flow of electrical activity along a specific trail of connected neurons through the forest. The wonderful and amazing characteristic of our brains is that we can create new pathways through the forest, and the old, unused pathways will grow over. This is called neuroplasticity, from the Greek word *plastos*, which means "moulded." We are literally sculptors of our own brain tissue.

When you repeat a thought, that faint trail in the forest becomes a discernible path, then a well-trodden trail, and eventually, a paved, easily accessible road. This process is summarized by the foundational principle of neuroscience, coined by Donald Hebb: "Neurons that fire together, wire together" (1949). The more your neurons communicate (fire), the stronger and more efficient the synaptic connection (wire) between them becomes. The more you walk a path in the forest, the more established it becomes.

This strengthening is called Long-Term Potentiation (LTP). This is how core beliefs are physically established: Years of repeated thoughts (e.g., *I am not good enough*) have created a deep, destructive pathway in the forest of your brain. These deep pathways are formed at the same time your young brain develops. When any external challenge arises, the brain defaults to this massive, well-paved path because it requires the least energy. The sum of these well-established pathways forms your thought norms, the habitual, automatic ways your mind interprets and reacts to the world. These are the pathways through the forest that are used the most because it's just easier to walk them. Our goal is to build a new set of thought norms (pathways) in your brain (forest), replacing the old, fear-based paths with resilient, adult, value-based superhighways.

If neural pathways can be strengthened through Long-Term Potentiation (LTP), they can also be weakened through Long-Term Depression (LTD). This brings us to the second vital neurobiological concept: neurological pruning. If you stop using a trail in the forest, the underbrush gradually grows back, making the path harder to follow. Neurological pruning is the natural process where unused or inefficient synaptic connections are weakened and removed. This ensures your brain remains efficient and capable of learning. Long-Term Depression is the process by which fewer people walk down the forest path, and pruning is the process by which those old pathways disappear.

To accelerate pruning and starve the old, bad, core belief pathways in your brain, you must deliberately withhold the energy that maintains them. Do not engage when a reactive thought arises (e.g., *"That was stupid, you are a failure"*), simply recognize it as "the old tape" and refuse to dedicate mental energy to its confirmation. The thought may arise, but the impulse to follow it must be ignored. The moment you catch the old thought, immediately shift your attention to an external sensory task (name five things you can see or four things you can feel) or, better yet, deploy the EDT.

The brain abhors a vacuum. You cannot simply *stop* thinking a thought; you must replace it with another, stronger thought. The core value action statement (*I validate my Integrity by taking ownership*) becomes the powerful replacement thought that actively strengthens the new pathway.

Your effort involved in this starving process is what gives your new, value-based pathway its initial strength.

The need for a quick, efficient response in times of stress is governed by the Hypothalamic-Pituitary-Adrenal (HPA) Axis, which is your body's central emergency response system. When your HPA axis is activated, it triggers the release of stress hormones. Chronic stress and reliance on fear-based core beliefs flood your system with cortisol and adrenaline, which is found to actually cause structural damage and shrink the window of tolerance (McEwen and Sapolsky 1995). This means that minor stressors in your life can trigger a high-cortisol response (e.g., the man's rude comment instantly sent me into flight/avoidance mode). The window of tolerance describes the optimal zone of nervous system function where you can function effectively and respond flexibly.

- **Narrow Window (Reactive):** The brain defaults to the massive core belief highways, leading to hyper-reactivity.
- **Wideness Window (Respond):** Your goal is to expand this window, enabling you to process difficult emotions without automatically sending your nervous system into emergency mode. You'll know your window of tolerance is widening when you can tell yourself, *"That would have really shaken me in the past."*

The EDT works by interrupting the automatic firing of your fear pathways when you are safe, thus physically protecting your brain from the chronic stress response and widening your window of tolerance. The EDT is a deliberate exercise designed to build new, resilient core value pathways in your brain and widen your window of tolerance.

Intervention 1: Conscious Interruption (Step 1 of EDT: Recognize Upset)

When a stressor hits, your limbic system — the ancient, emotional center of your brain — fires instantly. Step 1 (Recognize and Identify the Core Value being Challenged) forces the Prefrontal Cortex (PFC) to engage. We'll call this the forest ranger of your brain's forest, the center for logic, reason, and conscious choice. Activating your logic center (PFC/forest ranger) interrupts the immediate emotional hijack. Instead of automatically flowing down the old *I am flawed* highway, the signal is temporarily rerouted and slowed. This is the biological pause that creates space for choice. Think of your prefrontal cortex as the executive boss of your brain, the forest ranger, and the limbic system as the response team that will follow its own protocols but will listen to the prefrontal cortex if instructed.

Intervention 2: Value-Based Decision Making

To understand the EDT's power, we must examine the specific brain regions involved in automatic reaction versus conscious choice:

Brain Region	Function	Role in Core Belief (Automatic Response)	Role in Core Value (Conscious Choice)
Amygdala	Fear, Threat Detection – Your body's alarm system	Triggers an immediate HPA axis response; promotes "fight or flight" on the old pathway	Signal is noted but is rapidly overridden by the forest ranger (PFC) communication. Something is happening, yes, but there's no need for alarm.

Dorsolateral Prefrontal Cortex (dlPFC) the Boss/Forest Ranger	Cognitive Control – Executes the logical steps of a plan	Overridden by the amygdala; only works post-crisis to rationalize the behaviour	**The primary target of the Emotional Diagnostic Tool.** Used to hold the new core value action statement in working memory. It's the forest ranger instructing the response team to cool their jets.
Ventromedial Prefrontal Cortex (vmPFC) the Forest Ranger's Advisor	Decision Making – Assesses the emotional consequences of a choice	Avoids painful self-reflection, confirming negative self-concept	**Crucial for Self-Validation.** Engaged by Step 4 of EDT, it consciously reinforces the self-concept based on core values rather than external threats.

The EDT specifically engages your dlPFC and your vmPFC. By repeatedly engaging these regions, you are literally strengthening the pathways for conscious, value-based decision-making. You're building new, adaptive and helpful pathways in the forest of your brain.

Your conscious thought of the value and the subsequent realization of its integrity are your most powerful neuroplastic moments, solidifying new pathways in the forest of your brain. You are consciously asserting a new, empowering truth: *My worth is validated by my actions, not by external outcomes.* This is the act of firing the new neurons together. Every time you successfully self-validate, you physically strengthen the new core value trail. You are proving to the brain that this new path is a reliable route to inner peace. *Neurons that fire together, wire together.*

This is why repeating a statement as a mantra can be so powerful. With consistent use, this new, self-validated trail becomes the new default superhighway in the forest of your brain. Your brain learns that choosing the core value path is the most efficient, least stressful, and most rewarding route, thus widening the window of tolerance by lowering the threshold for automatic HPA activation. I don't want to give you the idea that the HPA axis isn't good for you; it is literally designed to save your life, like the airbags in your car. The problem is that, with a narrow window of tolerance, the airbag sensor can become overly sensitive, triggering the airbags even when no collision is imminent.

The science is clear: You are not a passive recipient of your brain structure; you are its architect. Your core beliefs are merely old paths, and your core values are the blueprint for the powerful, resilient new superhighways you can build. The challenge now shifts from understanding *why* you are reactive to practicing *how* you become responsive. Every moment of challenge, every perceived threat, is not a failure but a repetition in your neuroplasticity workout. Author Ryan Holiday (2014) advises that success is achieved not by luck or the inherent ease of the challenge, but by a consistent commitment to the process: preparation, patience, and persistence.

The difficulty of traversing your new core value trail is what gives it strength. With each conscious choice to deploy the Emotional

Diagnostic Tool, your old forest of limiting core beliefs begins to prune, and your new, abundant forest of core values thrives. Now that you understand the neurobiological necessity of building your new pathways, the final step is to apply them. The next chapter will guide you through the critical step of identifying and defining your personal core values.

CHAPTER 6

Identifying Your Core Values

YOU LEARNED THAT core beliefs are the automatic software installed during your childhood, and core values are the stable, self-validating hardware. You also discovered that the Emotional Diagnostic Tool is a mechanism for rewiring your brain, interrupting your old, fear-based pathways, and building new superhighways dedicated to peace and abundance.

Now, it is time to rewire your brain.

The first and most critical step in deploying the Emotional Diagnostic Tool (EDT) is identifying and defining your personal core values. You cannot defend a boundary you haven't defined, nor can you live authentically if you don't know what authenticity means to you. This chapter will guide you through selecting your personal set of core values, providing a list and exercise to help you uncover the fundamental principles that govern your life and your pursuit of inner peace.

When you define your values, you move them from vague ideals to tangible tools that can validate your self-worth in real time. The goal of this chapter is to narrow the vast list of possibilities down to your personal Top Ten Core Values. These will be the primary standards you use to reverse engineer your bad feelings by assessing challenges, making decisions and sustaining your state of self-empowerment.

Below is a list of 100 common core values, each with a brief description to help you determine if it resonates deeply with your intrinsic sense of self and integrity. As you read, highlight or mark any value that speaks to a behaviour or quality you feel is part of what makes you tick. You may already know some of your core values; use them, even if they're not on this list.

1. **Accountability:** Taking ownership of actions, outcomes, and responsibilities without excuses. This means accepting the results of your choices, whether positive or negative, and actively correcting missteps.
2. **Achievement:** A drive for accomplishment and the successful completion of goals. This value emphasizes setting high standards and consistently striving to achieve tangible results.
3. **Adventure:** Seeking new and exciting experiences; embracing the unknown with enthusiasm. It is the commitment to step outside one's comfort zone and embrace the risks and rewards of exploration.
4. **Affection:** Expressing warmth, care, and love through connection which is either platonic or romantic. It involves making a visible and genuine effort to show tenderness and emotional closeness to others.

5. **Ambition:** A strong desire to achieve success, power, or status. This value drives you to aim higher, work harder, and consistently push the boundaries of what you have already accomplished.
6. **Appreciation:** Recognizing the inherent worth and positive qualities in people and situations. It is the conscious practice of expressing thankfulness and noticing the good in one's life.
7. **Assertiveness:** Clearly and respectfully stating one's needs, opinions, and boundaries. This involves standing up for yourself without resorting to aggression or allowing others to dominate with impunity over yourself or others.
8. **Authenticity:** Living openly and truthfully in alignment with one's genuine self. This means acting without pretense, ensuring your outward expression matches your inner beliefs and values.
9. **Autonomy:** The freedom and capacity to make independent choices about one's life. It is a commitment to self-governance and to relying on one's own judgment and resources.
10. **Balance:** Maintaining equilibrium between one's professional and personal life. This is a conscious effort to allocate sufficient time and energy to all areas of one's well-being to avoid burnout.
11. **Beauty:** Recognizing, appreciating, and striving to create aesthetically pleasing environments. This value is expressed through a deep responsiveness to art, nature, and the visually appealing aspects of life.

12. **Belonging:** Feeling accepted, secure, and connected to a group or community. It is the need to feel fundamentally welcome and valued within a larger social structure.
13. **Boldness:** A willingness to take risks or defy convention; daringness in thought or action. This value provides the confidence needed to speak up and act decisively, even when it is unpopular or challenging.
14. **Bravery:** Confronting fear, pain, danger, or uncertainty with courage and fortitude. It is the strength to act despite fear, acknowledging the risk while still moving forward.
15. **Calmness:** Maintaining tranquility, composure, and emotional steadiness under stress. It is the practice of remaining centered and non-reactive, preserving inner peace amidst external chaos.
16. **Challenge:** Seeking out difficult tasks or situations that test one's abilities for growth. This is the appreciation for obstacles as opportunities to learn, expand, and prove capability.
17. **Clarity:** Striving for precision, coherence, and understanding in thought and communication. It involves eliminating ambiguity and ensuring that intentions and messages are perfectly understood.
18. **Collaboration:** Working effectively and jointly with others to achieve a shared goal. This value prioritizes collective effort and synergy over individualistic competition.
19. **Commitment:** Being dedicated to a person, course of action, or belief and following through on promises made to whom or whatever it may be. It is the reliability demonstrated

by seeing things through to their conclusion, regardless of difficulty.

20. **Communication:** The clear, effective, and empathetic exchange of information and ideas. This means mastering both speaking and active listening to foster mutual understanding.
21. **Community:** Fostering a shared spirit, support system, and collective identity with others. It is the desire to build and maintain strong social connections that offer mutual aid and encouragement.
22. **Compassion:** Showing sympathy and concern for the suffering of others, often leading to action. It involves recognizing shared humanity and being motivated to alleviate pain wherever one may find it.
23. **Confidence:** A firm belief in one's own abilities, judgment, and power. This internal conviction allows one to face difficulties without self-doubt or excessive hesitation.
24. **Connection:** Seeking deep, meaningful relationships and relational bonds with others. It is the commitment to vulnerability and intimacy that moves interactions beyond the superficial.
25. **Consistency:** Adhering to the same standards or principles over time; reliability in behaviour. This, one hopes, builds predictability and trust, making your actions dependable to yourself and others.
26. **Contribution:** Giving time, effort, or resources to help others or a greater cause. It is the drive to have a positive impact on the world that extends beyond one's immediate self-interest.

27. **Cooperation:** Working willingly with others for mutual benefit; shared effort. This involves setting aside personal agendas to align efforts toward a common, beneficial objective.

28. **Courage:** The mental or moral strength to venture, persevere, and withstand difficulty. It is the readiness to face the emotional discomfort necessary for ethical action or personal growth.

29. **Creativity:** Using imagination and original ideas to create something new and valuable. This is the capacity to solve problems in novel ways and generate innovative solutions or pieces of art.

30. **Curiosity:** A strong desire to know or learn something; an openness to exploration. This value fuels continuous inquiry and a playful engagement with the world around you.

31. **Decisiveness:** The ability to make firm, timely choices and commit to a course of action. This avoids procrastination and the paralysis of over-analysis, leading to effective action.

32. **Dedication:** Complete and wholehearted devotion to a task, cause, or person. It is the sustained focus and loyalty demonstrated by persistent effort toward a chosen objective.

33. **Dependability:** Being reliable, trustworthy, and consistent in fulfilling obligations. This is the quality of being counted on, ensuring your word is trustworthy and your presence is stable.

34. **Determination:** Firmness of purpose; continuing to work toward a goal despite obstacles. This is the unwavering resolve that refuses to quit or be deterred by setbacks.

35. **Discipline:** Training oneself to act according to established rules or principles; self-control. It is the practice of delayed gratification, prioritizing long-term goals over immediate impulses.
36. **Diversity:** Valuing the uniqueness of individuals from different backgrounds and perspectives. This is the commitment to inclusivity and the recognition that varied viewpoints strengthen outcomes.
37. **Empathy:** The capacity to understand and share the feelings of another person. It involves putting yourself in someone else's shoes to grasp their emotional reality and motivations.
38. **Empowerment:** Giving authority or power to others; the act of strengthening oneself or others. This is the deliberate act of fostering capability and confidence in those around you.
39. **Enjoyment:** Finding pleasure and satisfaction in activities, experiences, and daily life. It is the ability to derive genuine happiness and fulfillment from the present moment.
40. **Equality:** Believing in and advocating for the equal worth and rights of all people. This value demands fair treatment and opportunity for everyone, regardless of background or status.
41. **Excellence:** The quality of being outstanding or extremely good; striving for the highest standard. This means refusing to settle for mediocrity and consistently delivering superior results.
42. **Fairness:** Treating all individuals impartially and justly; adherence to equitable rules. This value ensures that decisions and distributions are unbiased and reasonable for everyone involved.

43. **Family:** Prioritizing and valuing close kinship, support, and blood or chosen relationships. This is the devotion to nurturing and protecting the bonds within one's immediate circle.

44. **Flexibility:** Willingness to change or compromise plans, ideas, or positions when necessary. This allows for adaptation to new information and unexpected circumstances without breaking one's resolve.

45. **Focus:** Concentrating attention on a specific task or objective; clarity of purpose. This is the mental discipline required to minimize distraction and maximize productivity.

46. **Forgiveness:** Choosing to let go of resentment or anger toward someone who has done wrong. This value frees the self from the burden of holding on to past hurts and grievances.

47. **Freedom:** The power or right to act, speak, or think without hindrance or restraint. This is the valuing of self-determination and the ability to choose one's own path in life.

48. **Generosity:** The quality of being kind and giving freely of time, money, or spirit. This value is expressed through a willingness to share resources without expectation of return.

49. **Gratitude:** The quality of being thankful; a readiness to show appreciation for what one has. This is the conscious recognition of blessings and the resulting positive outlook on life.

50. **Growth:** The process of personal development, improvement, and increasing capability. It is the continuous commitment to learning new skills and evolving one's perspective.

51. **Happiness:** A state of well-being and contentment characterized by positive emotions. This is the pursuit of joy and satisfaction through a balanced and fulfilling life.
52. **Harmony:** Living in a state of agreement, peace, and congruence with oneself and the environment. This value seeks balance and accord, minimizing internal and external conflict.
53. **Health:** The commitment to physical, mental, and emotional well-being — the essential resource for sustaining energy and living in alignment with all other values. This involves proactively managing nutrition, exercise, sleep, and emotional regulation.
54. **Honesty:** Adherence to the facts; being truthful in words and actions. This is the foundational commitment to speaking the truth and avoiding deception with oneself and others.
55. **Hope:** A feeling of expectation and desire for a certain thing to happen. It is the belief in a positive future outcome, even when present circumstances are difficult.
56. **Humility:** A view of one's own unimportance; freedom from pride or arrogance. This allows one to be teachable, acknowledge mistakes, and genuinely appreciate others' contributions.
57. **Imagination:** The faculty of forming new ideas, images, or concepts not present to the senses. This value encourages dreaming, envisioning possibilities, and transcending current reality.
58. **Improvement:** The act of making something better or the state of being made better. It is the steady, incremental progress made toward perfection or high quality.

59. **Independence:** Self-reliance and self-sufficiency; freedom from the control of others. This is the ability to sustain oneself and make decisions without external dependency.

60. **Initiative:** The ability to assess and begin things independently, taking the first step. This proactive value involves spotting needs and acting without being prompted or directed.

61. **Inner Peace:** A profound sense of tranquillity, serenity, and emotional stability within oneself. This is a non-reactive state where external conditions do not easily disrupt one' s core stability.

62. **Innovation:** The creation and successful application of new ideas, methods, or products. This value drives change and progress by challenging established norms and developing novel solutions.

63. **Insight:** The capacity to gain an accurate and deep intuitive understanding of a person or thing. It is the commitment to looking beyond the surface to grasp the true nature of a situation.

64. **Integrity:** Adherence to moral and ethical principles; being whole, honest, and undivided. This means doing the right thing even when no one is watching, ensuring internal consistency between beliefs and actions.

65. **Intuition:** The ability to understand something immediately, without the need for conscious reasoning. This is the trust in one's gut feelings or subconscious knowledge to guide decision-making.

66. **Joy:** A feeling of great pleasure and happiness that is often spiritually inspired. It is a deep, abiding state of delight and emotional lightness.

67. **Justice:** Upholding what is fair, proper, and equitable according to law and principle. This is a commitment to fairness and to the defence of the vulnerable and oppressed.

68. **Kindness:** The quality of being friendly, generous, and considerate toward others. It is the practice of goodwill and thoughtful action in all interpersonal encounters.

69. **Knowledge:** The facts, information, and skills acquired through experience or education. This is the intellectual pursuit of understanding and the continuous expansion of one's mind.

70. **Leadership:** The ability to guide, influence, and inspire a group toward a shared vision or goal. This involves setting direction, motivating others, and taking ultimate responsibility for the team's success.

71. **Learning:** The acquisition of knowledge or skills through study, experience, or being taught. This is a lifelong commitment to absorbing new ideas and self-improvement.

72. **Loyalty:** Giving firm and constant support or allegiance to a person, institution, or cause. This value demands faithfulness and dedication, especially in the face of adversity.

73. **Mastery:** Comprehensive knowledge or skill in a subject or activity. It is the dedication to achieving expert status and a deep proficiency through deliberate practice.

74. **Mindfulness:** The practice of intentionally focusing one's attention on the present moment without judgment. This is

the heightened awareness that creates emotional space and reduces automatic reaction.

75. **Openness:** Being receptive to new ideas, information, and experiences; being candid in communication. This involves maintaining a non-judgmental stance toward different viewpoints and being transparent.

76. **Optimism:** Hopefulness and confidence about the future or the success of something. This is the positive expectation that things will work out well despite current difficulties.

77. **Patience:** The capacity to accept or tolerate delay, trouble, or suffering without becoming annoyed. This value prevents impulsive action and allows for processes to unfold naturally.

78. **Peace:** Freedom from disturbance, conflict, or violence; a state of tranquillity and calm. It is the ultimate goal of internal stability and external non-aggression.

79. **Perseverance:** Persistence in doing something despite difficulty or delay in achieving success. This is the steady continuance in a course of action, a refusal to give up.

80. **Playfulness:** Engaging in lighthearted, spontaneous, and fun activities. This value promotes joy, reduces stress, and fosters creativity through non-serious interaction.

81. **Presence:** The state or fact of being deeply attentive to the current moment. This is the practice of showing up fully to give undivided attention to the people and tasks at hand.

82. **Purpose:** The reason for which something is done or exists; a sense of meaning. This provides direction, a "why" that fuels motivation and aligns actions with a greater goal.

83. **Resilience:** The capacity to recover quickly from difficulties; toughness and adaptability. This is the ability to bounce back from setbacks stronger and wiser than before.

84. **Respect:** Due regard for the feelings, wishes, rights, or traditions of others; self-regard. It is the fundamental acknowledgment of the inherent dignity and worth of all beings, including oneself.

85. **Responsibility:** The state or fact of having a duty to deal with something or having control over someone. This is the willingness to be the source of solution and action in one's life.

86. **Reverence**: A deep recognition of the intrinsic worth and sacredness of all living beings, encompassing both human and natural life. It is the commitment to act with profound respect, non-harm, and ethical care toward every form of existence.

87. **Security:** A feeling of safety, stability, and freedom from threat or danger. This value centers on establishing reliable foundations for one's physical and financial well-being.

88. **Self-Control:** The ability to manage one's emotions, desires, and impulses. This internal mastery allows one to respond deliberately rather than react impulsively.

89. **Service:** The action of helping or doing work for someone; contributing to the welfare of others. This is the dedication to improving the lives of others through direct action or support.

90. **Simplicity:** The quality or condition of being easy to understand or do; clarity and lack of complexity. This

values minimalism and focuses on what is essential, reducing clutter and unnecessary stress.

91. **Stability:** The state of being firm, steady, and not easily changed or disturbed. It is the reliability and solidity of character, emotions, and circumstances.
92. **Success:** The accomplishment of an aim or purpose; achieving desired results. This is the external manifestation of effective action and value-driven effort.
93. **Support:** Providing encouragement, assistance, or aid to another person or cause. This is the act of strengthening someone else through active help and emotional support.
94. **Teamwork:** Collaborative effort by a group of people to achieve a common goal. This values cooperation and the synergy that comes from effective teamwork.
95. **Temperance:** The practice of moderation, self-restraint, and disciplined control over one's own actions, appetites, and reactions. It is the commitment to finding balance and avoiding excess, ensuring that short-term desires do not compromise long-term values or well-being.
96. **Thoughtfulness:** Being considerate of others; careful and deep consideration of ideas. This involves anticipating others' needs and feelings before acting or speaking.
97. **Trust:** The commitment to reliability, integrity, and vulnerability, the foundation necessary to build secure relationships and foster self-confidence. This is the bedrock of all relationships, built by consistency between words and actions.

98. **Truth:** Fidelity to fact or reality; sincerity in action and character. It is the unwavering devotion to reality, whether pleasant or painful, as the basis for all action.

99. **Vitality:** The state of being strong and active; energy and a zest for life. This is the energetic expression of life force, encompassing physical vigour and mental alertness.

100. **Wisdom:** The active pursuit and application of experience, knowledge, and sound judgment to guide one's actions. It is the ability to see beyond the immediate situation, understand underlying truths, and make choices that serve long-term well-being and purpose.

The process of moving from this expansive list to your Top Ten is an exercise in self-discovery. This may stretch your mind a bit, but it's an essential step in rewiring your brain and building new pathways through the forest.

Phase 1: The First Cut

Reread the entire catalogue slowly. Highlight or circle every value that resonates with you, a value that, when you read it, makes you feel a slight internal affirmation: *"Yes, this feels like me."* Don't overthink this; go with your gut. Aim for a list of around 25–30.

Now, look at your highlighted list and ask yourself, "When I have experienced the most intense emotional discomfort or shame in my life (an intense argument with a loved one or when I disappointed myself in something I did), which of these values was being most severely challenged?" The values that, when violated, cause you the most internal pain are often your most important.

Based on the above, narrow your highlighted list down to twenty values. If you are struggling, group similar values (e.g., Mindfulness and Calmness) and choose the one that feels most foundational or descriptive of your internal ethical standard.

Phase 2: The Deep Dive

With your twenty core values in hand, it is time to reduce the list to your essential Top Ten. Write these twenty values down on a separate, clean sheet of paper and answer the following questions for each one:

> **Question 1:** "If I could only live by this one value for the rest of my life, even if it meant sacrificing all the others, would I be satisfied with the person I became?" (The answer should be a strong "Yes.")
>
> **Question 2:** "If I were absolutely certain I lived by this value every day, would I still need external praise or validation from others to feel worthy?" (The answer should be "No." If the answer is yes, the value is still probably tied to Esteem, not a true core value.)
>
> **Question 3:** "If I were forced to choose between this value and another essential value on the list, which one would be easier to sacrifice, knowing the other would define my life?" (The answer should take some time and even be difficult. Think about it, and if you answer well, you will know in your gut.)
>
> **Question 4:** "When I look back at the decisions I am most proud of in my life, which of these values was I acting on?" (This links your value to past positive actions, strengthening the new neural pathway.)

Use these four questions to rigorously prioritize and eliminate the values that are merely "nice to have" or tied to external rewards. Keep the values that feel essential to your inner compass and self-respect.

Once you have your ten core values, write them down on a clean sheet of paper. Keep this sheet of paper close by while you read the rest of this book, as you will need to reference your list often.

Phase 3: Defining Your Action Statements

Once you have your final Top Ten Core Values, the work of defining them begins. This is where you transform a noun (Integrity) into a self-validating instruction for your brain (Validation of the tool). Try to keep your action statements short and to one sentence. There's no right or wrong answer here; these are your identified core values. They may mean something different to you than to someone else, and that's okay. These are yours, and it's essential to identify what they mean to you personally.

For each of your ten values, complete this sentence:

I validate my core value of [Value Name] by [Specific, Controllable Action]

Examples:

- **Value: Respect**
    - **Action Statement:** I validate my core value of Respect by listening fully without interrupting and by maintaining my composure when I disagree with others, regardless of their tone.

- **Value: Authenticity**
    - **Action Statement:** I validate my core value of Authenticity by speaking my truth, even if it causes discomfort, and by refusing to pretend I am someone I am not.
- **Value: Perseverance**
    - **Action Statement:** I validate my core value of Perseverance by taking one intentional step forward in a difficult task every day, regardless of whether I feel motivated or whether the outcome is guaranteed.

Here are *my* ten core values and their action statements. They may mean something different to you than to me, and that's okay. This is just an example of what you should have on your sheet of paper when you have completed this part of the exercise.

Integrity – *I practice my core value of Integrity by doing what I say I'm going to do.*

Creativity – *I practice my core value of Creativity by creating art every day.*

Authenticity - *I practice my core value of Authenticity by living true to my core values.*

Empathy – *I practice my core value of Empathy by putting myself in others' shoes to see their perspective.*

Respect – *I practice my core value of Respect by respecting myself and others who are worthy of my respect.*

Health – *I practice my core value of Health by taking care of my mind, body and spirit.*

Truth – *I practice my core value of Truth by not lying.*

Trustworthiness – *I practice my core value of Trustworthiness by trusting myself, being trustworthy, and trusting others.*

Kindness – *I practice my core value of Kindness by being a nice human.*

Vitality – *I practice my core value of Vitality by living a full and adventurous life.*

By defining your value in terms of an action you control, you are telling the brain that the source of validation is internal, which cuts the strings of the external puppeteer. You are self-validating your worth based on your controllable *action*, not the uncontrollable *outcome* (e.g., the other person agreeing with you). Your action statements bring your core values into the real world for practical use. They are also the cheat sheet in relationships, which we will get into in a later chapter.

As your new neuropathways develop and your brain begins to use them by default, you may find that you only need two or three of your core values to guide you. This is because your other core values have become automatic and no longer require conscious validation.

Congratulations. By completing this chapter, you have moved from running on default, fear-based software to constructing a resilient, personalized operating system. Your Top Ten Core Values, armed with their specific action statements, are now the self-validated neural pathways you will forge in the coming chapters. This blueprint guides you through the practical application of the Emotional Diagnostic Tool. Keep the list of your 10 core values and action statements handy as we continue.

CHAPTER 7

Connecting Values to Emotional Reality

YOU WILL NOW calibrate your top 10 list by proving, through direct experience, the link between your core values and your emotional life:

Pleasure is a signal of value *stimulation*.

Discomfort is a signal of a value *challenge*.

We will begin with a powerful historical example of a core value holding steady under immense pressure. Then I will guide you through practical exercises to solidify this connection between your core values and emotions using your own life events.

Roman emperor and Stoic philosopher, Marcus Aurelius's life (reign 161 to 180 AD) was a testament to the fact that when your survival needs are threatened, an unwavering commitment to higher core values can maintain internal peace and effective action. Marcus Aurelius's reign was immediately shattered by the Antonine Plague, a pandemic likely caused by smallpox or measles, which began in 165 AD and lasted for fifteen years. It decimated the Roman army, destroyed the economy, and killed millions across the empire, threatening the very stability of Rome. The stress was compounded by simultaneous wars on the northern frontiers against German tribes.

Any leader's instinct in such a crisis is to panic, blame, or hoard resources, actions driven by the core beliefs of scarcity and fear. However, in his personal journals, *Meditations*, written during the final decade of his life between 170 and 180 AD, Marcus Aurelius documented a philosophy built upon a set of non-negotiable core values. These are famously known as the four cardinal Stoic virtues (Aurelius 2026).

Justice (Fairness) – The commitment to treat all people equally, govern for the benefit of all, and act with equity.

Temperance (Self-Control) – The ability to maintain composure, clarity, and rational thought under pressure; controlling impulses.

Wisdom (Truth) – The commitment to see reality clearly, without illusion or emotional distortion.

Courage (Endurance) – The ability to face fear, pain, or difficulty with fortitude.

When the plague struck, it violently challenged every lower-level need (Maslow's Safety and Esteem), but Marcus Aurelius's actions were dictated by his core values, demonstrating the self-filling fuel tank of abundance. The sheer scale of death meant farmland went untended and trade collapsed. Profiteering and hoarding became rampant, driving the cost of essential goods sky-high. The typical response of an insecure leader would be to impose crippling, fear-based taxes or seize assets to fund the war effort.

The threat was economic chaos and the violation of public trust. Marcus Aurelius refused to burden the desperate populace. Instead, he made an astonishing move in line with his self-validated value of Justice. He announced a public auction lasting several months, during which he sold off the entirety of his imperial estate: jewels, gold plates, silks, antique furniture, and even his wife's luxurious wardrobe (McLynn 2009). He raised massive funds, absorbed the financial pain of the crisis himself, and then used that money to finance the army and provide relief as much as he could. He governed with complete Justice, proving that his worth was validated by his adherence to ethical governance rather than by the accumulation of wealth or power.

As the death toll climbed, public hysteria spiralled. The Romans, desperate for a solution, demanded religious ceremonies, sacrifices, or a scapegoat for the catastrophe. The core beliefs of the populace, *"The gods are angry,"* and *"We need someone to blame,"* were running rampant. The threat was the collapse of rational thought and the temptation to seek easy, fear-based answers. While Marcus Aurelius placated the populace by overseeing certain religious rites (a political necessity), his private writings show a profound commitment to Wisdom (seeing things clearly). He refused to persecute minority groups, unlike many leaders before and after him. He focused on practical, actionable measures: importing physicians, organizing the sick, and maintaining civil order. He taught himself and his officials to distinguish between what was real (the disease) and what was opinion (the superstition), thereby validating his own inner clarity.

While the plague raged, the German Marcomanni crossed the Danube, initiating a brutal war that forced Marcus Aurelius to spend years on the unforgiving frontier (167–180 AD). This was a physical and psychological trial that broke most men. The threat was physical exhaustion, despair, and the impulse to retreat and hide in

Rome. Marcus Aurelius exercised severe Temperance and Courage. He lived as simply as his soldiers, enduring the gruelling climate and constant stress of warfare. He was there not because he wanted glory, but because his value of Responsibility (to the Empire) demanded it. His private practice of Stoicism was his daily emotional diagnostic tool, allowing him to accept the external events (the plague and the war) and focus only on the controllable response — his character and his duty.

The external events, plague, war, and economic collapse, were the ultimate obstacles. But by consistently choosing the core value script (Justice, Wisdom, Courage) over the core belief programming (fear, greed, self-preservation), he sustained his inner peace, achieved self-actualization, and earned his place as one of the most revered leaders in history.

This is the power you are preparing to unlock.

A common mistake people make is believing that happiness is a random occurrence. In reality, joy, peace, excitement, and contentment are specific, measurable biological responses to the stimulation of your core values. These positive emotions are your brain's reward system signalling: *"You are aligned. This is correct."*

Your first exercise is to intentionally connect the positive emotions of the past with the specific values from your Top Ten list.

Exercise A: Reverse-Engineering Joy

This is to show that your core values are the source code for your emotional fulfillment. There's no reason to reverse engineer when you feel happy. Just feel happy. The purpose of this exercise is to link the core values you identified with the emotion of feeling good.

1. **Recall a Peak Moment:** Think of a time in your life when you felt a profound sense of happiness, pride, or fulfillment. This should be a distinct, recent memory, or a time you felt that pure, authentic "Vitality."
2. **Describe the Action and Emotion:** Recall the event in detail, focusing on *what you did* and *how you felt* during that peak moment.
3. **Identify the Stimulated Values:** Now, look at your Top Ten Core Values from your sheet of paper. For the moment you recalled, ask yourself:
   - "Which of my values was I actively living or demonstrating in that moment?"
   - "Which of my core values is being stimulated?"

Example: Successfully launching a small, independent online business.
Emotion: Satisfaction, excitement, deep calm.
Stimulated Values:
1. **Autonomy:** I made all the decisions myself.
2. **Creativity:** I built something entirely new from an idea.
3. **Competence:** I used my skills effectively and solved complex problems.

When you can clearly trace a feeling of joy back to a specific action aligned with a core value, you gain a powerful insight: To replicate fulfillment, you do not chase the feeling by looking for external approval; the only person responsible for your happiness is you. Seek opportunities to validate your core values.

Just as pleasure signals alignment, sustained emotional discomfort (shame, anxiety, frustration, guilt, or the lingering feeling of dread) is your system's alarm bell. It signals that an external force or, more painfully, your own action, has challenged or violated a core value. You will address when your violation is internal and when there is no string to cut from an external puppeteer later in this book. Your next exercise is to intentionally connect emotional pain to the specific values being challenged.

Exercise B: Reverse-Engineering Discomfort

This exercise is the precursor to the Emotional Diagnostic Tool (EDT); you will use logic to trace pain back to its root.

1. **Recall a Lingering Upset:** Think of the most recent time you felt deeply upset, stressed, or ashamed by an event, and that feeling *stuck with you* for hours or days. This should be an event where somebody did something that really shook you, or you did something that you deeply regret doing. Maybe it was an interaction with a friend, coworker, or boss.
2. **Describe the Action and Emotion:** Think of the event, focusing on *what happened* (the external trigger) and the specific negative emotion (Shame, Guilt, Anger, Anxiety).
3. **Identify the Challenged Values:** Review your Top Ten Core Values. Ask yourself, "Which of my values was harmed or challenged by this event?" Be precise. Did the event challenge your Integrity (you lied) or your Respect (someone else was rude)?

Example 1: A friend promised to take you to the airport, but he was late, and you missed your flight.
Emotion: Anger, Betrayal, Disrespect

Challenged Values:

1. **Respect:** He didn't respect me and my need to catch the flight.
2. **Dependability:** He wasn't there when I needed him.
3. **Integrity:** He didn't do what he said he would.

Although your core values were challenged by your friend, remind yourself that these values are validated by you being Respectful, Dependable, and having Integrity. Your core values are intact. Let your friend be him, then you decide if you're ever going to depend on him again. But know that your core values are intact because you validate them through *your* controllable actions, rather than *his* action that you are not in control of.

Example 2: An argument where you yelled at your spouse over a trivial matter.
Emotion: Guilt, Remorse, Self-Anger

Challenged Values:

1. **Kindness:** I spoke harshly and violated my commitment to courtesy.
2. **Temperance (Self-Control):** I allowed my impulse (anger) to override my rational thinking.
3. **Communication (or Respect):** I chose yelling over clear, respectful dialogue.

Your pain tells you precisely what action is required next to repair your internal sense of self-worth. If you yelled, the required action is an apology (an affirmation of Kindness/Respect), not simply wallowing in guilt, doing nothing, and hoping the problem just goes away. This may further challenge other core values you have, resulting in perpetual issues that fester.

By successfully completing these exercises, you have practiced the essential first step toward cognitive distancing and emotional intelligence in calibrating your core values.

Connecting the Stimulus and the Challenge

Emotional State	**Neural Signal**	**Interpretation**
Positive Emotion (Joy, Pride, Peace)	VmPFC Activation (Self-Validation)	**Stimulation:** You acted in alignment with a core value. **Action Required:** Repeat the value-congruent action. If it feels good, keep doing it.
Negative Emotion (Shame, Anger, Anxiety)	Amygdala/HPA Axis Alarm	**Challenge:** An action (yours or another' s) violated a core value. **Action Required:** Deploy the EDT to resolve the conflict and self-validate the value.

Think of this as your secret weapon against those toxic lies we all tell ourselves, like, "I'm just not good enough." Usually, when you feel something like shame, it just feeds that old, negative belief and makes it stronger.

But this is where your *forest ranger*, that part of your brain that stays calm and observes, comes to the rescue. Instead of letting that shame spiral out of control, you use your conscious mind to stop it in its tracks. You look at that feeling and realize it's actually a signal that one of your values, like Integrity, was just stepped on or challenged.

By doing this, you're shifting the focus from "I am a flawed person" to "My Integrity was threatened." That change in perspective is significant because it gives you a clear exit ramp. Instead of sitting in the shame, you take an action that proves your Integrity is still alive and well, whether that's an apology, a confession, or making a firm commitment to do better next time.

Every time you choose that action over the old shame spiral, you are paving over a bumpy road and building a neural superhighway. You're training your brain that peace through values is the way to go, rather than getting stuck in the mud of those old beliefs.

Eventually, things that derailed you in the past won't even upset you, as you will automatically recognize what's really happening. This is an exercise in "taking a step back" and thinking before responding.

CHAPTER 8

Step 1 of EDT: Recognize Your Upset, The Power of Cognitive Distancing

DID YOU KNOW that the average person experiences approximately 6,200 thoughts per day, and that a significant majority of them are simply repeats of those from the day before? (Mittal et al. 2020).

This fact reveals the challenge and the necessity of Step 1 of the Emotional Diagnostic Tool (EDT): to interrupt your mind's automatic, repetitive thought patterns that make you feel bad and consciously engage the command center of your brain (dlPFC-the forest ranger). You have defined your core values and linked them to when you feel great and when you feel bad. Now, you must implement the first, and often most difficult, step of the EDT: *Recognize when you feel bad and name it to tame it.* This step is not just about identifying an emotion; it is about creating a deliberate, neurological gap between you (the self) and your thought/emotion (the event). This gap is called cognitive distancing, and mastering it is the foundation of emotional self-empowerment. Without this distance, you may remain trapped in the reactive programming of your old operating system.

It's important to distinguish the difference between metacognition and cognitive distancing. *Metacognition* is "thinking about your thinking." It is the higher-order awareness that you have a mind, and that your mind is currently producing thoughts, feelings, and judgments. The concept is being the internal observer. When you realize, *"I am having a lot of anxious thoughts right now,"* you are practicing metacognition. The thought allows you to monitor, evaluate, and regulate your mental state. In trauma work, metacognition is what allows a client to notice their nervous system activating before they spiral into a flashback.

Cognitive distancing is a specific metacognitive strategy. It is the active process of stepping back from a thought to see it as a "subjective mental event" rather than an absolute truth. If metacognition is *noticing* the thought, cognitive distancing is *changing your relationship* to it. Instead of being "inside" the thought (immersed), you view it from the outside (distanced). This thought breaks the automatic link between an activating event and your reactivity. It's like the boss of your brain, the forest ranger, stepping in to tell your emergency response system to think a bit before pulling the alarm. For a first responder, distancing is the skill that allows them to see a chaotic scene and think, *"This is a high-stress situation,"* or *"This isn't my emergency. I'm okay,"* rather than *"I am in danger and I'm going to fail."* Compartmentalizing the chaos is a required skill for emergency workers so they can perform their work in highly stressful environments. Processing the event usually happens after the call or when they're back home after their shift.

To put it simply: *Metacognition is the ability. Cognitive distancing is the action.*

Feature	Metacognition	Cognitive Distancing
Role	The broad ability to observe your mind	A specific technique to create space.
Question	"What is my mind doing right now?"	"Is this thought a fact or just a mental event?"
Analogy	Being the director of a play	Moving from the *stage* to the *audience*
Goal	Awareness and self-regulation	Reduced reactivity and objectivity

Metacognition provides the *awareness* that someone has entered your "value bubble" and is causing friction. Cognitive distancing gives you the tool to separate your identity from that friction. It allows you to say, "My core value of Respect is being challenged, but I do not have to react with anger to defend it." When you combine the two, you move from *emotional immersion* (where you *ARE* your anger) to *observation* (where you *HAVE* anger, but you *ARE* your values). The focus of Step 1 of The EDT is cognitive distancing, separating yourself from the challenge.

When your core value is challenged, whether by external criticism or an internal mistake, your automatic alarm system (amygdala–HPA Axis) may be activated, flooding your system with cortisol and adrenaline. This high-stress state is designed by evolution to make you react *now*, not think *later*. In this state of high emotional arousal, your thoughts and feelings fuse into a single, overwhelming reality. You don't just *feel* shame; you *are* shame. You don't just *have* the thought, "*I am a failure,*" you *believe* you are a failure. The core belief highway automatically takes over, and your prefrontal cortex is temporarily muted and told to step back while the emergency is dealt with. But with effort, you can say, "No, I'm not stepping back; I'm in control here."

Think of it like this: You don't have to think about breathing, but you *can think about it.* You can consciously interrupt some of your body's automatic systems. By achieving cognitive distancing, it becomes easier for you to interrupt the automatic response your body has to protect you when you are actually safe. It's the calm presence among the perceived chaos of you willingly not breathing.

The Emotion Wheel, often attributed to psychologist Robert Plutchik (1980), provides a structured framework for identifying your emotions. It works by moving from a core, primary emotion (the center of the wheel) to more nuanced, secondary and tertiary emotions (the outer rings). When you feel upset, pause and locate your feeling on the wheel, moving outward from the primary emotion in the center until you find the most specific term. The diagram below is not Robert Plutchik's Wheel of Emotions, but this version better suits our needs for this book.

How to Use the Emotion Wheel for Cognitive Distancing

1. **Start Central:** Identify your core primary feeling: Anger, Fear, Bad, Sadness, Happy, Disgust, or Surprise. (When distressed, you will likely be in the Anger, Fear, or Sadness sectors).
2. **Move Outward:** If you feel Anger (center ring), scan the next ring: Are you feeling *Bitter, Mad, Aggressive, or any of the other emotions listed in the wheel?*

3. **Identify Nuance:** Move to the outer ring. If you chose *Mad*, are you feeling *Furious* or *Jealous*?

Example: Instead of "I don't feel good," you move from Sad to Depressed to Empty.

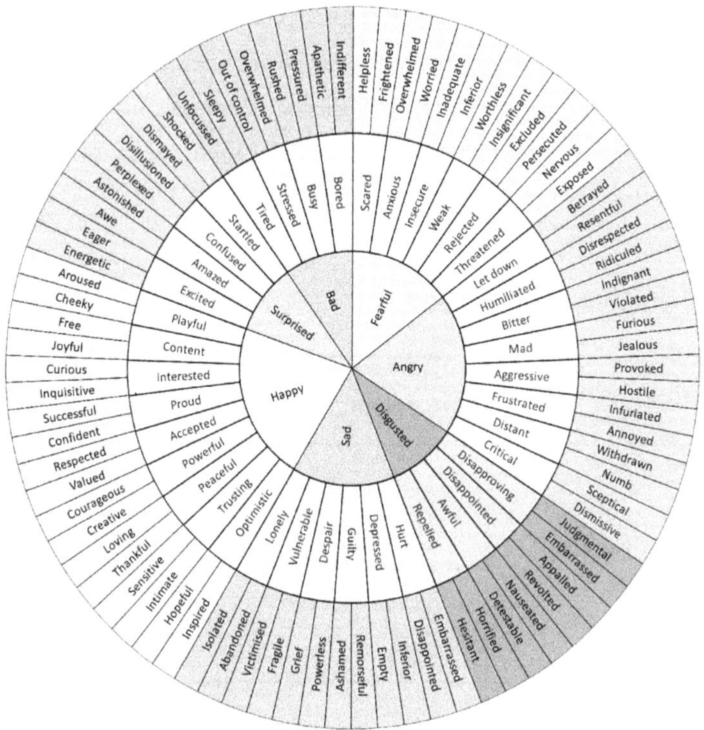

This process is not just vocabulary building; it is a neurological intervention. By forcing this procedure, you're exercising your logical processing center (dlPFC), effectively telling your nervous system: "If I can name this feeling with such specificity, I am not in immediate danger, and the thinking part of my brain is still in control." *Name it to tame it.*

Cognitive distancing is the disciplined act of forcing the control center of your brain to engage and override your amygdala's signal to set off your body's alarm system. When you are not practicing cognitive distancing, you may fall into automatic, often irrational, thinking patterns known as cognitive distortions. These biased ways you perceive reality can potentially be the destructive output thinking patterns of your maladaptive core beliefs. Understanding these distortions helps you recognize the content of the "old tape" that Step 1 of the EDT aims to silence. I use this list to help my clients "Name it to Tame it," which allows them to transition from "I am this ..." to "This is a thought I'm having."

Cognitive Distortions

Distortion	**Description**	**Example (Core Belief Output)**
All-or-Nothing Thinking	Viewing situations in black-and-white, polarized terms (perfection or total failure)	"I made one small mistake on the report, so the entire project is ruined, and I am a complete failure."
Overgeneralization	Drawing a sweeping, global conclusion based on a single piece of evidence or event	"My presentation went poorly today. I am terrible at public speaking, and I will always be."
Mental Filter	Focusing exclusively on the negative detail while ignoring all the positive context	You receive a promotion but dwell only on the one piece of negative feedback from your review.

Disqualifying the Positive	Rejecting positive experiences by insisting they "don't count" for some reason	"They only complimented me because they were being nice, not because I actually did a good job."
Jumping to Conclusions	Making a negative interpretation without solid evidence (e.g., mind-reading or fortune-telling)	"My partner hasn't replied to my text; they must be angry at me and planning to leave."
Catastrophizing	Exaggerating the importance of negative events or minimizing positive ones	"If I miss this deadline, I will be fired, my career will be over, and my family will hate me."
"Should" Statements	Criticizing yourself with "shoulds," "oughts," or "musts," leading to guilt or anger	"I should be able to handle this stress easily. I shouldn't have gotten angry."
Emotional Reasoning	Assuming that because you *feel* something, it must be true	"I feel inadequate, therefore I *am* inadequate."
Personalization	Blaming yourself (or others) for events and outcomes that you had no control over	"The team lost the contract because I didn't work hard enough, even though I was only responsible for a small part."

Cognitive distancing can be an immediate countermeasure to these distortions. The moment you acknowledge you're in a bad mood, you're doing something powerful: You're yanking that thought out of the *autopilot* lane, where things get distorted and messy, and moving it into the *observer* lane. You stop *being* the emotion and start *watching* the emotion, which lets you observe the situation for what it actually is. You are labeling the thought as a mental event *before* it can solidify into a false truth.

To fully understand the urgency of Step 1of the EDT, we must examine your nervous system's automated response through the lens of Stephen Porges's Polyvagal Theory (2011). This theory demonstrates *why* your window of tolerance — how much you can take before you react — shifts so dramatically under stress. The Polyvagal Theory states that your autonomic nervous system (ANS) has an internal "hierarchy of response" based on how safe you feel. This is regulated by the Vagus Nerve, a nerve that, when stimulated, puts you in a calm, relaxed state.

To help understand the theory, first imagine you are in this scenario:

The air hung crisp and cool, carrying the clean, pine-scented breath of the deep woods. You were deep in the embrace of the weekend, nestled at the edge of a pristine mountain lake with your closest friends. The campsite was a masterpiece: Canvas tents stood rigid in the twilight, and the fire pit glowed with a hypnotic, amber intensity. Around the circle, the conversation flowed like the gentle stream nearby, deep, honest, and meaningful, punctuated by easy laughter and the occasional, perfectly timed strum of one of your friends' softly played acoustic guitar.

You felt a profound, almost luxurious sense of peace. The ritual was perfect: the sticky warmth of roasted marshmallow melting on your tongue, the clink of glasses, and the vast, silent tapestry of the stars overhead. It was this effortless connection, this absolute detachment from the world's demands, that you craved and found here. In this moment, under the expansive sky, you were completely present, utterly safe, and perfectly content.

Then, the world shattered!

It was an instantaneous, violent intrusion that tore the fabric of your peace. From the impenetrable black wall of the old-growth timber, a monstrous form erupted. A giant grizzly bear, a dark, hulking leviathan of muscle and fur, sprang into the periphery of your firelight.

The collective gasp of the group was swallowed by a single, seismic sound: The bear reared up on its hind legs, dwarfing the campfire, and let loose a bone-chilling roar. It was a physical wave of pure, predatory intent that vibrated through your chest and rattled the stones beneath your seat.

In the sudden, terrifying silence that followed, every instinct you possessed screamed. The world narrowed to the enormous, black eyes of the predator, and you realized, with a sickening drop in your stomach, that you were the closest. The bear's head lowered slightly, its focus locking onto you. Time stretched, agonizingly slow, as you watched the massive shoulders coil and the heavy paws lift off the dirt.

The bear lunged.

Every neurological alarm in your body fired simultaneously. The fight-or-flight response surged, but before your muscles could engage, the magnitude of the threat, the sheer impossibility of escape, forced the ultimate survival response: You froze. Your heart, which moments ago had been beating a gentle rhythm of peace, seemed to seize in your chest, leaving you a statue of paralyzed terror directly in the path of the oncoming beast. Your body and nervous system prepared for death.

This horrifying scenario illustrates the components of Porges's Polyvagal Theory.

Safety – Ventral Vagal Complex (VVC): Sitting at the campfire, chill, relaxed, and engaged in deep and meaningful conversation.

> The newest vagal pathway. This is the state of safety and connection and the state where your core values are best expressed. Your prefrontal cortex is online, your window of tolerance is wide, and you can engage in social interaction (empathy, listening, connection). This is the goal and where you want to be most of the time.

Fight or Flight – Sympathetic Nervous System (SNS): The bear jumps out of the trees.

> The middle pathway. This is the state of mobilization (fight-or-flight) and where your alarm system kicks in, your HPA axis and hormonal surge take over. The energy is directed away from your thinking brain, the prefrontal cortex (PFC), and toward your survival. This happens automatically, as it should, because you don't want to spend the time thinking about the situation before your nervous system engages. Most of your cognitive distortions above are created here.

Freeze – Dorsal Vagal Complex (DVC): You know the bear is going to kill you.

> The oldest vagal pathway. This is the state of immobilization (freeze or collapse). This is your survival response that's triggered when both your Chill/Calm (VVC) and Fight/Flight (SNS) fail (e.g., profound shame, helplessness). This is why some people freeze during high-stress events and don't run away from danger or defend themselves.

When a perceived challenge arises, but you are still physically safe, your system may still automatically shift from the VVC (Safety) to the SNS (Fight/Flight). Recognizing your upset and knowing there is no danger and that you are safe is the conscious act of sending a signal back to your nervous system saying, "Stop! This is not a life threat. I am safe enough to think."

By forcing the logical recognition and labelling of your emotion (cognitive distancing), you recruit the the control center of your brain, the forest ranger, which in turn acts as a soothing influence on your Vagus Nerve, the cranial nerve that calms you down, allowing your system to move through the Polyvagal ladder toward the state of safety and connection, thereby widening the window of tolerance.

The concept of cognitive distancing resonates deeply with Carl Jung's (1968) theories on the conscious and unconscious mind. Jung argued that you don't see the world exactly as it is; you see it through a set of "mental glasses." These mental glasses are tinted by everything you've been through (your core beliefs) and the deep-seated, universal patterns of the human mind (what he called Archetypes). Because of this, your reality isn't a direct broadcast but instead is a version of the world filtered and coloured by the glasses you're perceiving your life with. Jung's work suggests that you primarily perceive your world *through* this. Your core beliefs are not just thoughts; they are the fixed colour and distortion of the lens you constantly wear.

If your "mental glasses" is the set of glasses you use to see the world, then your forest ranger, the thinking boss of your brain (PFC), is the one who realizes those glasses are dirty. Think of it like this: When you're in a bad mood, your lenses are often covered in the smudges of old memories or the tint of a negative core belief. Without the forest ranger, you just assume the world really is that dark or blurry and don't realize the problem is the glasses themselves.

When you are experiencing a shame spiral, the core belief (*I am a failure*) has taken over the lens, making the entire world filtered through failure. You are so fused with these glasses that you cannot tell the difference between the distortion and what is actually happening.

Cognitive distancing, in the Jungian context, is the first moment you realize you have these glasses, and, more importantly, that you have an eye capable of taking the lens off and examining it. The development of the "eye" (the conscious observer) is the path to individuation, Jung's term for achieving psychological wholeness and self-realization. The eye is your highest self, aware of the subconscious distortions (the core beliefs) but not ruled by them. This transition from being fused with your mental glasses to observing it is the fundamental prerequisite for Emotional Intelligence (EQ), as popularized by Daniel Goleman (1995). Goleman's model of EQ starts with Self-Awareness, the accurate recognition of one's emotions, strengths, weaknesses, and values.

- **Low EQ:** You are a puppet to your core beliefs. You are *in* the emotion and, therefore, cannot manage it.
- **High EQ (The Goal):** You can recognize an emotional state as it arises, differentiate between the feeling and your reality, and choose a value-based response. Think of Keanu Reeves's character, Neo, taking the red pill in *The Matrix*; he becomes aware of what his reality actually is.

Step 1 of the EDT, Recognize Your Upset, is the disciplined practice that builds your foundational Self-Awareness. It is the action of saying, "I am not Anger; I am merely observing Anger." It's taking the lens you're perceiving your reality through off and checking for smudges.

To help deploy Step 1 of the EDT, you can take the high-level idea of stepping back from your thoughts and turn it into a practical, physical habit that actually changes how your brain is working in the moment. This is a five-second moment of conscious effort that interrupts the automatic neural flow in your brain.

Let's think of a scenario where this plays out: You see a shocking response to a social media post you made that derails you.

The Reaction: You feel a flush of heat, a knot in your stomach, or an impulse to fight or run.

The Action: Physically stop moving. Freeze your fingers over the keyboard or your mouth mid-sentence.

The Scan: Quickly run an inventory of your body. *Where* do I feel this upset? Is it a tightness in my chest? A headache? Identifying the physical location grounds your emotion in your body, making it feel less like a global threat and more like a localized sensation. This will ground your emotion in the physical reality, ensuring you are responsive, not reactive.

Once you've stopped the physical reaction, you can label the internal experience. This is the anti-distortion measure where you intentionally separate the *I* from the *feeling*.

"This is the worst thing that has ever happened. I can't handle this."

↓

"I am observing the feeling of panic."

↓

"I am having the thought that I can't handle this," or "My body is registering a strong impulse of anger."

You can now decide what to do from a position of responding rather than reacting. Write a reply, ignore the comment, or delete and block the person.

To further starve the old neural pathway (pruning), you can thank the core belief for its effort before dismissing it. This is a powerful form of non-resistance and confirmation of your safety. Silently say, *"I recognize my automatic response and how it is designed to protect me from failure, but I choose to handle this with my value of Competence."* This acknowledgement validates the *intention* of the old core belief (survival) but negates its *authority* over your current and new thought patterns. It is a decisive move toward the new, value-based pathway. This is giving yourself a break and expressing some self-compassion.

Imagine you are in a meeting with several colleagues, and your boss criticizes a report you spent days compiling. He's standing, arms crossed, staring at you in a room full of your coworkers and waiting for a response. Your stomach drops. The core belief *I am not competent* fires. You immediately become defensive or you shut down (Dorsal Vagal Freeze), confirming the feeling of incompetence. (Alarm system engaged, your heart rate goes up, you start to feel warm, and you get a knot in your stomach.)

Cognitive Distancing Response

1. **Physical Stop-and-Scan:** You pause your impulse to interrupt. You feel the heat in your ears and the tightness in your throat.
2. **Conscious Labelling:** You label your sensations and think, *"I am observing a strong feeling of shame and the thought that I am a failure (All-or-Nothing Thinking)."*
3. **Distancing:** You realize, *"That feeling is not me. It is just an emotion triggered by a perceived threat to my value of Competence."* (Vagus nerve is stimulated, window of tolerance widens.)
4. **Action Prep:** You are now calm enough to proceed and respond to your boss's criticism rather than react to it. You are thinking before responding.

When you use this brain hack, you are putting the logical part of your brain back in the driver's seat. You have removed the distorting lens of your perception and are now viewing the situation with your objective, rational "eye." Most importantly, you are now in a better position to respond to your boss's criticisms.

The hardest part of Step 1 of the EDT is not the technique, but the resistance you feel against changing what's familiar to you. Your old core belief pathways feel easy and comfortable, even if they lead you to pain. Your mind will try to pull you back into the emotion because it is *used* to the shame, anger, or anxiety; it's familiar. Remember, your brain isn't designed to keep you happy; it's designed to be efficient at providing for your survival. It doesn't care how you feel about it. Eventually, situations like the one described with your boss won't require conscious cognitive distancing, as it will happen automatically due to the new neural pathways you build by exercising the EDT. It's like riding a bike: It's tough to get going, but once you get momentum, it's easy.

Your commitment to the EDT is a commitment to being less reactive in situations that cause temporary unease. Your discomfort of consciously pausing and labeling the emotion is short-term; your reward is the long-term relief from the anguish caused by your fusion with maladaptive core beliefs. This chapter has provided you with the conceptual and neurological tools to execute *Step 1 of the EDT – Recognize your upset.* In the next chapter, you will leverage this newfound cognitive distance to implement *Step 2 – Identifying the precise core value from your list that has been challenged.*

CHAPTER 9

Step 2 of the EDT: Identify the Core Value Being Challenged

IN CHAPTER 8, you mastered the critical first step of the Emotional Diagnostic Tool: Name it to Tame it — Recognize and Name your Upset by applying cognitive distancing. You learned to separate yourself (the observer) from the emotion/thought (the observed event), disrupting the automatic emergency response that puts you into a state of fight-or-flight (HPA axis and the sympathetic nervous system). You intentionally put down the distorted "lens" of your maladaptive core beliefs. Now, with your alarm signal successfully paused and observed, you move to Step 2, the heart of the EDT: Identify the Core Value Being Challenged.

This step turns your vague feeling of "upset" into actionable information that you can process. By connecting your specific emotional distress to a particular core value you have, you shift from victimhood (being controlled by the emotion) to sovereignty (analyzing the emotion).

While Marcus Aurelius provides the historical gold standard for maintaining philosophical values under existential threat, a modern example from the world of celebrity can illustrate how core values provide a shield against the intense pressure of public criticism, a common external challenge in the digital age.

Ryan Reynolds, known for his relentless output of media and business ventures, often faces the challenge of perpetual public scrutiny, commercial failures, and the risk of oversaturation. His core values, which appear to be humor (Self-Deprecation) and Authenticity (Transparency), are his primary tools for navigating these challenges. In 2011, *The Green Lantern*, a massive, $200 million film in which Reynolds starred, was a notorious critical and commercial failure. For another actor whose core beliefs might have centred on Esteem or Perfection (Maslow's lower tiers), this public failure could have led to years of shame and defensive blame, the typical output of catastrophizing or all-or-nothing thinking.

Instead, Reynolds continually deployed his core values as a shield and a mechanism for self-validation.

Challenged Value: Achievement/Competence (publicly questioned).

Core Value Response: Reynolds did not deny the failure (affirming Authenticity), but immediately diffused the emotional tension with self-deprecating humor. He has consistently mocked the film over the years, incorporating the failure into his later, highly successful *Deadpool* franchise, such as one scene where Deadpool travels through time to kill the actor before he signs the contract for *Green Lantern*.

By turning the colossal, shame-inducing failure into a joke, Reynolds successfully:

1. **Limited External Access:** He preempted critics. If he already jokes about it, their criticism loses its power.

2. **Affirmed His Values:** He validated his core values of Humor and Authenticity: His worth is defined by his ability to be honest and find the joke, not by box-office success.

His worth, like the self-filling fuel tank, was sustained internally by his adherence to his values rather than the external outcome of the movie. This ability to instantly shift from emotional fusion ("I am a failure") to cognitive distance ("This is a funny failure that I can use") is the essence of recognizing when you feel bad (Step 1 of the EDT) and the basis for identifying your challenged value (Step 2 of the EDT).

Once you have successfully achieved cognitive distancing (Step 1: "I am observing the feeling of anger"), you must immediately engage your rational processing center, the forest ranger of your brain (dlPFC), to conduct the analysis for Step 2: Identify the Core Value Being Challenged. Review your list of 10 core values from chapter six and identify which are being challenged. The process is simple, yet requires intense focus on the distinction between the external trigger causing the upset and how it's making you feel:

1. **Isolate the Emotion (use the emotion wheel if needed):** What is the primary feeling? (e.g., Shame, Anger, Anxiety, Guilt).
2. **Isolate the Trigger:** What specific event caused this feeling? (e.g., the boss criticized the report, I yelled at my spouse, I missed a deadline).
3. **Trace the Violation:** Check your list of core values: "Which of my core values was challenged by this event?"

There is a common trap called Emotional Reasoning, a cognitive distortion, in which your brain tells you, *"I feel like a failure, so I must be a failure."* This lie will try to stop you from identifying the core value on your list.

That's why you have to identify the value being challenged quickly; you're trying to train your brain to take a new, healthier path. If you skip Step 1 (stepping back to observe), you'll try to find your values while you're still tangled up in those old, toxic beliefs. It's like trying to read a map while you're spinning in circles; you need to stop spinning first before the map makes any sense. This will become easier as the new thought process, new pathways in the forest, gets established in your brain:

Be cautious of the *Fusion Response:* "I feel terrible, so the value that's challenged is my Worth." ("Worth" is the core belief. It's too broad and leads to a defence of the ego, not an action of the value.) Work toward the *Distanced Response:* "I am observing intense guilt. That guilt is tied to the fact that my own behavior violated my commitment to honesty when I lied to my colleague." (This is actionable and leads to self-validation.)

Using your predefined action statements gives you a quick way to check whether you have identified the true core value. If the action statement associated with the identified value had *prevented* the upset, you've found the root. The power of identifying your challenged core value relies on the successful use of cognitive distancing which comes from taking a step back and recognizing that you are *experiencing* the feelings rather than *being in* the feelings.

Acceptance and Commitment Therapy (ACT) provides strong validation for why this separation is so vital. ACT suggests that much suffering stems from psychological inflexibility, the inability to shift perspectives and take value-driven action when rigid thoughts (such as core beliefs) take over (Hayes et al. 1999).

ACT Process	EDT Step	Function in creating new pathways in your brain (neuroplasticity)
Defusion	**Recognize Your Upset**	Separating the self from the thought, interrupting the emergency response signal (Amygdala/HPA)
Acceptance	**Labeling Your Upset/Value**	Acknowledging the thought/feeling/challenge without fighting it
Identifying Values	**Identify Your Core Value**	Creating and reinforcing new thought patterns
Committed Action	**Self-Validate**	Taking action in line with defined values, self-filling your fuel tank (self-empowerment)

In Step 2 of the EDT, you choose to let your values guide you. Instead of trying to push the painful feeling away, you simply acknowledge it by saying, “I’m noticing that I feel guilty.” Immediately, you use that feeling to find the root cause. You ask yourself which of your values was challenged or ignored. For example, instead of just sitting in a bad mood, you realize, “I feel guilty because I wasn’t honest.” This turns the uncomfortable emotion into a helpful signal that tells you exactly what needs attention.

Research across therapeutic models consistently shows that the ability to adopt a detached observer stance is the key to emotional regulation. They also show that when you can reframe a thought as, “This is my mind thinking a thought,” rather than, “This is the truth,” the physiological stress response (measured by skin conductance or heart rate variability) is reduced (Fledderus et al. 2013). The effect is simple: distance equals dampening. When you realize that you are separate from your thoughts, you effectively turn down the volume on your brain's emergency alarm (the limbic system). By immediately checking your list of top ten core values, you keep that alarm from getting louder. By the time you've traced your feeling back to a specific value, the initial panic has already started to fade. This gives your logical brain the quiet it needs to think clearly and make a wise decision without your emotions getting in the way. You're learning to respond rather than react.

Let's return to the example of the man who criticized my dog Dexter.

Step 1: Recognize the Upset

- **The Reaction:** You feel a flush of anger, a tightening in your chest, and the thought: *What's wrong with this person? He has no right to judge me.*
- **The Intervention (Cognitive Distancing):** You pause. You silently label: *"I am observing a feeling of intense anger and the strong thought that he is a terrible person" (All-or-Nothing Thinking).* You detach from the anger. Carl Jung would say this is you taking off glasses through which you perceive this event and looking at it objectively.

Step 2: Identify the Challenged Value

- **The Diagnostic Question:** Which of my core values is being challenged by this man's action? Check your list.
- **The Tracing:** You quickly scan your Top Ten list.

    - Was my Integrity violated? *No, I told the truth.*
    - Was my Authenticity violated? *No, this is an issue with him, not me.*
    - Was my Respect violated? *YES.* His action (harsh, unprovoked criticism) violated my standard of how people should interact, and the threat triggered a feeling of powerlessness, which challenged my Kindness.
- **The Conclusion:** The core values being challenged are Respect and Kindness.

The moment you identify your true core value(s), the nature of the challenge changes. It is no longer about disproving the man's opinion (an external, uncontrollable task). It is now about affirming your value of Respect (an internal, controllable task). The focus shifts immediately from the external puppeteer to your internal value system. This distinction is the cornerstone of self-empowerment: moving from needing the world to change for your validation to choosing your actions to validate yourself. The next step in the tool requires you to analyze the source of the challenge to prepare for the crucial self-validation phase.

CHAPTER 10

Step 3 of the EDT: Identify the Source of the Challenge

IN THE PREVIOUS chapters, we laid the scientific groundwork: you defined your core values and learned the crucial initial move of cognitive distancing. You used this distance to precisely identify the specific core value from your list that has been challenged. Now we arrive at the fork in the road. Step 3: *Identify the Source of the Challenge, Internal or External.*

This distinction is perhaps the most critical analytical step in the Emotional Diagnostic Tool (EDT), as it determines what you're going to do next. The goal of this chapter is to give you the clarity to correctly identify the "puppeteer pulling the strings of your values." Is it an external figure whose string you can cut, or is the challenge coming from within?

Before diving into the mechanism, it is essential to reinforce what happens in your brain during this process. The deliberate, methodical thought process you are engaging in, pausing, labeling, tracing, and diagnosing, is the physical act of building your new, value-based superhighway in the forest of your mind. Every time you choose to deploy the EDT, you are:

Strengthening the dlPFC (The Forest Ranger): The dorsolateral prefrontal cortex, the region for cognitive control and complex analysis, is being exercised.

Weakening the Amygdala's Authority (The Alarm System): The emotional reaction is being rerouted.

Establishing the New Default (Making New Paths through the Forest): The more you utilize this structured thought process, the wider, more established, and more efficient this new pathway will become. Eventually, the brain will default to this path, and the old core belief pathways will naturally grow over through neurological pruning, removing the unused pathways.

The more you utilize this thought process, the wider and more established the pathway in your brain (forest) will be. This deliberate repetition is your neuroplasticity workout. Often, I hear from my clients who have adopted this method that situations that used to challenge them no longer do. By building this new pathway in the forest of your brain, you are creating a shield against external factors that used to derail you. Your brain will default to the new internal validation pathway over time.

The hardest part about figuring out why you're upset is that people are messy. Usually, something happening *outside* of you triggers a reaction *inside* of you. For example, if a stranger is rude to you (external), it might trigger an old, painful thought, such as "I'm not respected" (internal). To get clear, you have to ask: Where did the problem actually start? Was it the other person's behaviour, or is it coming from your own inner beliefs? Think of it like a "who started it?" investigation.

- **The External Challenge:** Someone else crossed a line or acted poorly
- **The Internal Challenge:** Your own brain recycling an old, negative story about yourself

Distinguishing between the two is vital because you can't "fix" the rude stranger, but you can absolutely manage how your internal forest ranger handles that old story.

The challenge is external when the *violating action* was committed by someone or something outside of your control. This is the external puppeteer.

Violating Action: Someone else's conduct (criticism, rudeness, breaking a promise)

The Goal: To affirm your self-worth based on your adherence to your values, regardless of the external outcome. You cannot control the puppet master, but you *can* control whether their actions compromise your internal peace.

Examples: The man who judged me for walking my dog in his cart challenged my core value of Respect. A colleague fails to deliver their work, violating your value of Dependability. A harsh critique threatens your sense of Competence.

If you could magically make the other person behave differently, would your immediate upset disappear? If yes, the primary challenge is external.

This is the biggest trap that keeps people stuck in a loop of stress and letdown: the belief that other people *must* change their behaviour before you can feel good about your own values.

For example, if your partner criticizes you, an old and unhealthy voice in your head might whisper, "If they actually respected me, they wouldn't say that. I can't be at peace until they stop." When you think this way, you're basically handing someone else the remote control to your emotions. You've given up your Internal Locus of Control — your power to decide how you feel — and surrendered your emotional independence.

Instead of being the boss of your own peace, you've made your happiness a prisoner of someone else's choices. Let's look at how this plays out with a value like Joy or Happiness in a relationship:

- **The Trap:** "I can only feel respected if you stop criticizing me." If they fail, they are violating your value, and you feel justified in your disappointment (giving your power away).
- **The Truth:** "I value Respect, so I will act with respect and set boundaries, regardless of how you choose to behave" (keeping your power).

Expecting the external puppeteer to change for your benefit can be a recipe for chronic dissatisfaction because it delegates the validation of your most important internal standards to the ever changing and contradictory will of people you meet. The EDT's work is to cut the string of the external puppeteer and bring the validation home.

The challenge is internal when the *violating action* was committed by you, resulting in a direct violation of your own standards. This is the internal puppeteer, the part of you acting against your higher core values.

Violating Action: Your own conduct (lashing out, lying, procrastinating, breaking a boundary you set for yourself)

The Goal: To take specific, corrective action to repair your internal sense of self-worth. **Examples:** You yelled at your spouse, violating your Kindness and Temperance. You procrastinated until the last minute, violating your Discipline. You knowingly exaggerated a fact, violating your Integrity.

If you could magically undo your last action, would your immediate upset disappear? If yes, the challenge is internal.

Most challenges involve a mix, which is why the diagnosis must focus on the *root* cause of the *lingering* pain.

Scenario	Step 1 (Identify the Upset)	Step 2 (Challenged Value)	Step 3 (Source)
Simple External	Anger, Frustration	Respect	External: A stranger was rude to you.
Simple Internal	Guilt, Remorse	Honesty	Internal: You told a lie to avoid conflict.
Complex	Shame, Anxiety, Guilt	Discipline (internal) and Dependability (external)	External caused Internal: A colleague missed a deadline (external), causing you to rush and make a serious mistake (internal violation of Discipline).

In the complex situation, even though your coworker started the fire, the reason you still feel "burned" (that lingering shame) is usually because you feel like you let your own standards slip. You might stop being mad at them fairly quickly, but you're still stuck feeling disappointed in yourself. To move past this, you have to focus on what *you* can fix. You can't change how your coworker acts, but you are 100 percent in charge of rebuilding your own sense of Discipline. A great way to picture this is by thinking about the previously mentioned external puppeteer.

The external puppeteer pulls the strings of *everyone else's* actions, words, and opinions. This puppeteer is uncontrollable, irrational, and motivated by factors entirely separate from you and may have very little to do with you. Perhaps the man who judged Dexter and me on our walk did so because he had an argument with his partner and went for a walk to blow off some steam, making Dexter and I collateral damage.

You believe that if you just pull the string hard enough, through arguing, pleading, or demanding, you can force the external puppeteer to change and validate your value. This rarely works. Instead, the goal is to cut the string between the puppeteer and your internal value. The string you cut is the expectation that the puppeteer must change and validate your core values for you. Your self-validation will be: "I uphold my value regardless of the puppeteer's behaviour." The man judging how I walk my dog cannot violate my Respect if I affirm my Dignity by refusing to engage with him.

The internal puppeteer holds the strings of your own impulses and actions. This puppeteer is governed by unconscious, fear-based maladaptive core beliefs (e.g., "I need external approval, so I must not procrastinate to avoid failing"). The internal puppeteer is you.

When the challenge is internal, the goal is to take control of the hand that holds the strings. The string you must control is the impulse to violate your own values. Your self-validation will be: "I repair my value through immediate corrective action." If you violated Kindness by yelling, the corrective action is an apology and a plan for restraint, not simply arguing that the yelling was justified. The apology isn't for the benefit of the person you yelled at, it's to repair your challenged core value of Kindness.

This distinction between internal and external challenge is deeply rooted in psychological research, primarily the concept of Locus of Control (LoC), developed by Julian Rotter (1966).

External LoC: Belief that outcomes are controlled by outside forces (fate, luck, other people). This mindset reinforces maladaptive core beliefs and may lead to a sense of victimhood and learned helplessness. Fusion with the external puppeteer.

Internal LoC: Belief that outcomes are primarily the result of one's own efforts, choices, and actions. This mindset aligns with the core value OS. Taking control of the internal puppeteer (yourself).

The EDT is designed to help you move toward an internal locus of control. By correctly identifying the source of the challenge, either external or internal, you are explicitly acknowledging:

If External: "I accept I cannot control the external event (LoC). My action must be internal" (Self-Validation).

If Internal: "I accept I *am* responsible for this event (LoC). My action must be corrective and self-affirming" (Self-Validation).

To illustrate the extreme power of this internal vs. external distinction, we turn to the experience of psychiatrist Viktor Frankl, the founder of logotherapy and a survivor of the Holocaust (2006). Frankl was imprisoned in concentration camps during World War II. In this environment, every external factor — safety, food, family, freedom, and health — was controlled by the most malicious external puppeteer imaginable, the Nazis.

- **The External Challenge:** The Nazis violated every human value: Dignity, Respect, Life, and Autonomy.
- **Frankl's Core Value:** Meaning (or Purpose) and Freedom (internal choice).

Frankl's core insight was: *"Everything can be taken from a man but one thing: the last of the human freedoms, to choose one's attitude in any given set of circumstances, to choose one's own way"* (2006).

When the guards stripped him of his family, his clothes, his medical notes, and his wedding ring (external challenge to Respect and Love), Frankl deployed the diagnostic thought process:

Recognize Upset: *I am observing profound grief and despair.*

Identify Value: *The challenged value is the Love for my wife and my Purpose as a psychiatrist.*

Source: External: The violation came entirely from the guards.

Value-Driven Response (Internal Action): Frankl mentally reconstructed his lecture notes and spent hours imagining giving his future lectures on logotherapy. He mentally retreated to the image of his wife, conversing with her in his mind.

He knew he could not stop the guard (external LoC), but he could *choose his attitude* (internal LoC). By choosing the internal action of reaffirming his values of Love and Purpose, he successfully cut the external string, preventing the shame and despair from consuming him. He self-validated his worth, not through survival but through the consistent exercise of his inner freedom.

By correctly identifying the source in Step 3 of the EDT, you prepare for the crucial final steps of the Tool:

If the Challenge is...	**Your Focus is:**	**Outcome:**
External	**Self-Containment.** Affirming your core value by focusing on your internal perspective and response. You can't control what other people do or think.	You feel self-empowered by successfully cutting the external string that pulls on your sense of value and by validating your worth independent of external events.
Internal	**Corrective Action.** Affirming your core value by immediately repairing the violation through a controllable action.	You achieve Self-Control by acknowledging and managing internal strings, strengthening the neural pathway by self-validating your challenge value through repair.

CHAPTER 11

Step 4a of the EDT: The External Challenge

IN THE PRECEDING chapters, you armed yourself with the first three steps of the Emotional Diagnostic Tool (EDT):

Step 1: Recognize the Upset (Chapter 8).
Step 2: Identify the Core Value (Chapter 9).
Step 3: Identify the Source (Chapter 10).

This chapter is the climax of the EDT: deploying your personalized action statements to manage external stress and cut the string between the person or event that challenged you and your internal self-worth. When the challenge is external, your goal is to validate your value system without demanding change from the uncontrollable, external world.

When you get a "like" on social media, or a compliment from someone else, or are otherwise validated by someone else, your brain's reward center, specifically a tiny area called the nucleus accumbens, lights up with dopamine. This is the same feel-good chemical that fuels other addictive behaviours. As Sherman et al. (2016) pointed out, this makes external approval feel like a drug. The danger is that your sense of self-worth becomes hooked on these outside signals, leaving your happiness at the mercy of how other people react to you. This neurochemical reality affirms the danger of your external puppeteer: You are biologically wired to seek validation from the tribe. When a stranger's action, a rude comment, a dismissive look, a nasty comment on social media, or a hateful critique challenges one of your core values, your brain can register the drop in social standing as a biological threat. Your core beliefs may scream, *"I am not safe until they validate me!"*

The goal of Step 4a is to break a bad mental habit that your brain has become addicted to. Instead of letting your mood depend on what others do, you are rerouting your brain's reward signal to a different area called the ventromedial prefrontal cortex (vmPFC). Think of the vmPFC as the closest advisor to the forest ranger of your brain. It is the part of your brain that decides what actually matters to you and allows you to feel good about yourself based on your own standards, instead of someone else's.

To fully appreciate the health of your core value OS, it is worth examining its opposite: the narcissistic personality structure. Individuals with severe narcissistic characteristics are often described as being locked entirely into the external locus of control. Research suggests that, in narcissistic individuals, the internal reward system associated with authentic self-reflection and connection is often underactive or disorganized (Jauk et al. 2017). Individuals with high narcissistic traits often show reduced gray matter volume in the vmPFC. Their sense of self must be continually inflated by external supply, praise, adoration, or dominance. They may not have the neurobiological capacity to self-validate, or it is challenging for them to do so.

Narcissist is a label often used to criticize an individual's character. People diagnosed with Narcissistic Personality Disorder (NPD) who meet the DSM-5-TR's requirements for that diagnosis require help and treatment like anyone else who has a mental health condition. It's not a character flaw most of the time; it's a biopsychological condition that requires treatment. Just because your partner or friend is a self-centred jerk doesn't necessarily mean they are a narcissist.

- When a narcissist's value of Superiority is challenged by a slight criticism (external stressor), it's challenging for them to self-validate. It's difficult for them to say, "I value my competence, and my competence is fine regardless of this critique," and actually believe it.
- Instead, they must force others to repair their internal deficit, often through rage, deflection, or gaslighting.

This is the psychological dead end you are trying to avoid and where the discipline of *self*-validation comes in, ensuring that your emotional stability comes from within rather than external sources.

It will be rare for a single external event to challenge only one of your core values. A professional setback, an intense family argument, or a public snub can pull at several of your strings simultaneously. For example, an unjust termination (external) can challenge your Competence, your Security, and your Respect, leading to a chaotic blend of shame, fear, and anger.

When the challenge is confirmed as external, the action is internal and self-empowered. You shift your focus away from the external puppeteer's string and use your action statements as a mantra to redirect the flow of self-worth. For each challenged core value identified in your core value list, complete the following powerful three-part sequence:

1. *My value of [value name] has been externally challenged.*
2. *I validate my core value of [value name] by [specific, controllable action] …*
3. **Sovereignty Statement:** … *and others can do as they wish without challenging my core values.*

This short, focused action is the moment you stop letting the world push you around and firmly grab the steering wheel of your own life. The final step, the sovereignty statement, is rooted in what author Mel Robbins calls *The "Let Them" Theory* (2024). The core idea is simple: Stop exhausting yourself by mentally fighting, policing, or persuading others to behave in ways that make *you* feel safe or validated.

Let them be rude. Let them be late. Let them misunderstand you. Let them criticize your creativity. Let them make decisions you disagree with. These are the choices of the external puppeteer, and they are outside your control. The freedom gained by releasing the need to control others is channelled into empowering yourself through self-validation of your core values. Let *them* be them, but then let *you* respond in alignment with your values.

The key to this theory is recognizing that external actions reflect *their* internal state; they are not a decree about *your* worth. When you say, "Others can do as they wish without challenging my core values," you are stating a psychological fact: Their choices have no jurisdiction over *your* validation of core values.

Example 1: The Rude Colleague

Scenario: A colleague publicly undermines your work in a team meeting, suggesting your ideas are amateurish and incomplete.

Tool Step	Action
Step 1: Recognize Upset	I am observing intense, sharp *anger* and the thought of catastrophizing (I'm horrible at my job).
Step 2: Identify Value	Check your top 10 list. The challenged values are Respect and Competence.
Step 3: Identify Source	The source is external.
Step 4: Self-Validate	**1. (Respect): Action Statement:** *I validate my core value of Respect by maintaining my composure and treating others with courtesy, even when they fail to do so …* and others can do as they wish without challenging my core values.
	2. (Competence): Action Statement: *I validate my core value of Competence by reviewing my work meticulously and seeking objective facts to affirm my skill …* and others can do as they wish without challenging my core values.

The feeling of rage defuses. You acknowledge the colleague's choice of words ("let them"), and you pivot to the controllable self-validation ("let you"). You have successfully cut the puppeteer's string and can now respond instead of react.

Example 2: The Late Partner

Scenario: Your romantic partner is chronically 30 minutes late for dates, which challenges your value of Reliability.

Tool Step	Action
Step 1: Recognize Upset	I am observing *frustration, disappointment*, and the thought of Personalization ("They don't care about me").
Step 2: Identify Value	Check your top 10 list. The challenged value is Reliability.
Step 3: Identify Source	The source is external (the partner's action of being late).
Step 4: Self-Validate	**Action Statement:** *I validate my core value of Reliability by being a reliable person and by adhering strictly to the boundaries I set* … and others can do as they wish without challenging my core values.

You shift from demanding change from your partner to empowering your own choices. You accept their lateness ("let them") and then affirm your own value ("let you") by controlling your *response* to their lateness, removing the power of their actions to obstruct your internal peace. Next time, you will tell your partner to be ready 30 minutes before the actual time. When you place a boundary on someone else's behaviour, the action isn't a demand for a change in what they do; it is simply the action you take as a result.

Example 3: The Airplane Etiquette Challenge (A threat to Respect and Empathy)

You're sitting in the window seat on a plane. The flight isn't full, so the person sitting in the aisle seat moves across the aisle, but the person sitting next to you, in the middle seat, doesn't move over.

Tool Step	Action
Step 1: Recognize Upset	I am observing *disappointment* and *annoyance.*
Step 2: Identify Value	Check your top 10 list. The challenged values are Respect and Empathy.
Step 3: Identify Source	The source is external (Why isn't this guy moving?)
Step 4: Self-Validate	**1. (Respect): Action Statement:** *I validate my core value of Respect by maintaining my composure and treating others with courtesy, even when they fail to do so* ... others can do as they wish without challenging my core values.
	2. (Empathy): Action Statement: *I validate my core value of Empathy by being able to put myself in the shoes of others and trying to see the situation from their perspective* ... and others can do as they wish without challenging my core values.

The feelings of annoyance and disappointment dissipate because your dignity has been protected internally. You are not reliant on the passenger to validate your empathy. This self-validation is a conscious choice of perspective anchored in your defined values. This actually happened to me on a recent flight. I asked myself, "Should I ask him to move?" "It wouldn't have been an issue if the person in the aisle was still there." "He clearly doesn't care that he's sitting next to me." I chose to leave it and practice validating my core value of empathy. I later realized he was sleeping when the aisle person moved. About 30 minutes later, when he woke up, he moved. If being true to your core values means waking the person and asking them to move, then do that. Remember, it's okay for each of us to have a different list of core values and to practice living by them.

Choosing to validate yourself isn't about ignoring reality or pretending a problem doesn't exist. Instead, it's about deciding to see the situation through the lens of your own values. By doing this, you stop wasting your mental energy trying to change or control other people, an effort that rarely works anyway, and you put that energy back where it belongs: on yourself.

- **The Old Way:** You spend your "battery power" trying to force others to understand you, respect you, or change their minds.
- **The New Way:** You use that same power to stay true to your own standards, regardless of what others do.

If the Challenge is External...	The Demand (Core Belief) is:	The Choice (Core Value OS) is:
Violation of Boundaries	"They *must* respect my boundaries."	"I will affirm my boundaries by setting the required limit, and I validate my worth by the act of doing so, regardless of their reaction."

Violation of Fairness	"The situation *must* be fair for me to be okay."	"I will validate my Integrity by acting with Fairness myself, and I will accept that I cannot control external injustice. Let them be unfair."

The final, essential part of cutting the strings is actually *saying it.* Whether you whisper it in private or state it clearly in your mind with total focus, the act of putting your choice into words helps wire this new habit into your brain. According to research (Lupker et al. 2020), this kind of verbal reinforcement helps strengthen the new neural pathways you are trying to build. When you recite a statement like, "*I am honouring my value of Respect by staying calm … others can do as they wish,"* you activate the language centers of your brain. By using language, you force your forest ranger (the dlPFC) to stay in charge. This deliberate move bypasses your brain's automatic "panic button" and tells your body to stop wasting energy on stress and start moving toward a state of calm and control.

Verbalization works by turning a thought into a declarative statement, thereby increasing your perceived reality and power. It provides the self-referential validation that your vmPFC, the valuation center, needs to register a positive outcome, effectively giving yourself the "feel good hit" of self-respect.

The external challenge is a test of your self-empowerment. The stress you feel is a byproduct of the major flaw: believing your emotional state is dependent on the choices of others. By using the four steps and concluding with the powerful sovereignty statement (let them), you accomplish cutting the external puppeteers' string:

Old OS (Core Beliefs)	New OS (Core Values)
Core Error: Expecting others to change for my benefit	**Core Truth:** Others can do as they wish without challenging my core values.
Action Plan: Demand others change (Argument, Pleading, Blaming)	**Action Plan:** Self-validate the challenged value using the action statement (Calmness, Choice, Perspective).
Result: Chronic emotional stress, disappointment, and a narrowed window of tolerance	**Result:** Emotional independence, peace, and a widened window of tolerance

You have now learned a technique to respond to the world's chaos. It will take time for this new way of thinking to take hold, and the pathway in your brain forest begins to widen. You're building new pathways through the thick forest; it will get easier the more you use them. The next, and arguably more profound, challenge is addressing the enemy within. Or what happens when you have taken your power back through your action statement, but the bad feelings don't go away? Chapter 12 will pivot to managing the internal challenge, where the puppeteer is *you*, and the solution requires corrective action, not mere choice.

CHAPTER 12

Step 4b of the EDT: Radical Acceptance

IN CHAPTER 11, you learned how to respond to external chaos by using your action statements to cut the puppeteer's string, a profound act of self-validation and internal sovereignty. But what happens when you look down and realize you are the puppeteer?

This is the internal challenge, and it triggers the most destructive emotions: shame, guilt, and remorse. This chapter details the final step of the Emotional Diagnostic Tool, when the source of the challenge is you, or when taking back your power from external sources doesn't make you feel any better. The Radical Acceptance framework can help you navigate the negative emotions that remain even when you take your power back.

In 2024, I was privileged to be invited as the keynote speaker for a national nursing conference in Gatineau, Quebec. The topic I chose was Post-Traumatic Growth, and the 90-minute presentation I designed included several dramatic, hospital-based artworks I created under my artist name, DanSun. This was a big event, with nearly 1,000 nurses in attendance.

I arrived hours early to ensure all technical components were flawless. The technical team confirmed my presentation was loaded from my USB drive.

"Any video or audio in your presentation?" they asked.

"Nope," I replied, "two fewer things to go wrong."

They smiled in agreement. As the ballroom filled, I became really excited. This is what I live for. The moment arrived: the host delivered a wonderful introduction, music played, and I walked onto the stage. The sheer energy of the room stimulated my core value of Vitality, a zest for life and living to my fullest capacity. I was nervous, but excited to get started.

I began my introduction by stating the necessary disclaimers for the potentially triggering artwork in the presentation and emphasizing the importance of stepping into pain to achieve growth. As I flipped the slides, I froze.

The slides did not match what I had prepared.

It felt as though the blood drained from my face. In that instant, I realized I had handed the technical team the wrong USB drive, one from a completely different presentation I had recently given. I didn't know what slides were coming next. That nightmare most of us have had of being naked in front of a large crowd suddenly became my horrifying reality. I couldn't stop. The build-up was too incredible, and everyone was already engaged. I decided to continue. As artwork I created of sports medicine trainers started popping up on the two massive screens, the horror intensified. I realized this was a 30-minute presentation I had given at a sports medicine conference in Montana the week before. I needed to fill 90 minutes on Post-Traumatic Growth, but I was working with material that was only a third of the required length. My stomach dropped even further.

I ended up ad-libbing for the entire 90 minutes, drawing heavily on my clinical and public speaking experience.

They loved it. They gave me a standing ovation and rebooked me for another event. But I felt absolutely horrible! I wanted to pack my bags and run. I let the organizers know what had happened, and they kindly dismissed my grave error, but that internal feeling persisted.

My core values of Authenticity and Integrity were *smashed*. I hadn't provided the service I promised, despite the positive feedback. My old core beliefs, established in childhood, that I am not good enough and feel insignificant (I'm the youngest and most introverted of three), were confirmed and reinforced, so no wonder I felt so horrible.

The Emotional Diagnostic Tool for the Internal Challenge:

1. **Recognize the Upset:** I am observing overwhelming Shame and Guilt (using the Emotion Wheel to specify beyond general *Sadness*).
2. **Identify the Core Value:** Integrity (I failed to deliver the promised material) and Authenticity (I believed I failed to be true to who I actually am).
3. **Identify the Source:** Internal (My own failure to use the correct USB drive, my own momentary panic).

The solution to this shame required radical action to repair my sense of self-worth. When your Core Value challenge is internal, the goal is to repair the internal connection that *you* broke. The shame and guilt may persist until the necessary repair is made. Your path to repair is dictated by the Four Paths of Radical Acceptance, a concept rooted in Dialectical Behaviour Therapy (DBT) and Stoic philosophy (Linehan 1993). Radical acceptance teaches that for any painful, uncontrollable situation, be it an external tragedy or an internal failure, you have four choices for how to respond:

Option 1: Fix the Problem (The Direct Path)

This is the best choice when you actually have the power to fix what went wrong. It is the fastest way to get your values back on track.

- **What to do:** Take an action that matches the value you ignored. For example, if you lied (hurting your value of Integrity), you fix it by confessing and telling the truth. If you put off a task (hurting your value of Discipline), you fix it by getting to work right now.
- **The Goal:** To prove to yourself that your values, not your lazy or fearful impulses, are the ones calling the shots.

In the world of radical acceptance, this is the problem solving stage. You are actively using your hands and mind to change the reality of the situation, because, in this case, it *can* be changed.

Option 2: Shift Your Perspective (The Mindset Change)

This path is for the times when you can't change what happened. Maybe you made a massive mistake that can't be undone or you experienced a loss that can't be recovered. Since you can't change the past, your only move is to change how you talk to yourself about it.

- **What to do:** Look for a different way to see the situation. You choose a mindset that hurts less and helps you grow more. Instead of seeing the problem as a dead end, you see it as a lesson. You turn the obstacle into your instruction manual.
- **The Goal**: To find a purpose for the pain. You prove to yourself that even if you didn't do a great job (Competence), you are still becoming a smarter, deeper person (Wisdom) because of it.

This aligns with the idea that while you cannot change the facts, you can change your relationship to them. By accepting that the event happened and choosing a helpful way to view it, you stop the pain you cause yourself by fighting reality.

Option 3: Leave the Situation (The Exit)

This is your "break glass in case of emergency" option. You use this when a situation is deeply painful and cannot be fixed or improved, like an abusive relationship or a toxic job that is making you physically ill.

- **What to do:** You completely cut ties and walk away from whatever is causing the pain.
- **The Goal:** To prove that you value your own Safety or Self-Respect enough to set a permanent boundary. You are deciding that your well-being is more important than staying in a bad situation.

This option shows that radical acceptance doesn't mean you have to stay and suffer. It means you clearly see the situation for what it is (toxic and unchangeable) and accept that the only way to honour your values is to remove yourself entirely from the environment.

Option 4: Do Nothing and Suffer (The Automatic Trap)

Without using the tools to step back and analyze your feelings, it's easy to fall into this trap without even realizing it. Most people on this path stay stuck because they are waiting for someone else to change or apologize before they allow themselves to feel better.

- **What happens:** You let the shame take over. You replay the mistake in your head over and over, eventually believing the lie that you are worthless or not enough.
- **The Goal:** There isn't one. This isn't a choice; it's a total surrender that leaves you emotionally paralyzed. *This* is the path we want to avoid at all costs.

In radical acceptance theory, this is known as willfulness. It's the opposite of acceptance. Instead of dealing with reality, you fight it or hide from it, which only turns your initial pain into long-term suffering.

To choose Option 1 or 2, you must understand the distinction between the two primary internal emotions:

- **Guilt:** *I did something bad.* Guilt is action-oriented and repairable. It focuses on the behaviour, not the self.
- **Shame:** *I am bad.* Shame is identity-oriented and paralyzing. It reinforces the core beliefs.

The entire process of the Emotional Diagnostic Tool (EDT) is designed to convert the emotion of Shame into the motivating emotion of Guilt, which can then be addressed by one of the four options of the radical acceptance theory.

Reframing is simply a way to change your perspective (Option 2). It is a powerful way to heal when you feel you've violated your own code of ethics or when you experience Moral Injury — we will talk about this in just a moment. When you can't undo a mistake, like my Gatineau slides disaster, you can use two specific mental shifts to heal:

- **Time Reframing (Temporal):** Change how long you look at the problem. Instead of seeing this failure as a permanent brand on your character, imagine yourself five years from now. By then, this disaster will likely be a valuable lesson or even a funny story you tell. Looking at the big picture of your life makes the pain feel much smaller and temporary.
- **Value Reframing:** Change how you define winning. If you failed at your original goal (like Discipline), stop beating yourself up over that specific metric. Instead, look at how you handled the fallout. Did you show Courage by facing the music? Did you show Temperance by staying calm under pressure? By measuring yourself against the values you *uphe*ld during the crisis, you can find a way to respect yourself again.

Reframing doesn't change the facts of what happened, but it changes the weight those facts carry. It moves you from being a *failure* in the present to being a *student of life* with a long-term future.

To avoid falling into Path 4 (Suffer), allow yourself some Self-Compassion. Self-compassion is *not* letting yourself off the hook (which would violate Integrity), but rather acknowledging that everyone makes mistakes before moving to corrective action. You treat yourself as you would a valued friend who made the same error.

Since I brought up moral injury, I would now like to distinguish it from PTSD. We will discuss trauma more in Chapter 16. While post-traumatic stress disorder (PTSD) is fundamentally rooted in fear and the perception of a threat to one's physical survival, Moral Injury (MI) is psychological and spiritual distress resulting from persistent distress that arises from a personal experience that disrupts or threatens: (a) one's sense of the goodness of oneself, of others, of institutions, or of what are understood to be higher powers, or (b) one's beliefs or intuitions about right and wrong, or good and evil (VanderWeele et al. 2025). A recent study by VanderWeele et al. introduces the notion of "moral trauma" as a spectrum encompassing moral injury and moral distress.

	Post-Traumatic Stress Disorder (PTSD)	**Moral Injury (MI)**
Persistent reexperiencing of the traumatic event	Yes	May or may not
Avoidance of trauma-related stimuli	Yes	May or may not
Fear	Yes	May or may not
Concern over some action or experience related to moral valuation or worth	May or may not	Yes

Treated with Prolonged Exposure Therapy as a preferred approach to treatment	Yes	Will not be especially helpful for treating moral injury if the questions of guilt, shame, or betrayal are not addressed.
Impaired prefrontal cortex and overactive amygdala (Disconnection between your brain's forest ranger and your emergency response system)	Yes	No

(VanderWeele et al. 2025)

For individuals whose professions are based on a profound commitment to service, such as military personnel, first responders, and healthcare providers, MI often results from impossible ethical choices or betrayals by trusted leadership, leaving behind powerful feelings of guilt, shame, and betrayal (Litz et al. 2009). The distress in MI is not triggered by a fear of death, but by the violation of one's own *moral* core values, the internal code that defines their worth and their humanity. Understanding the difference between the two conditions is important for effective recovery and for applying the core value OS correctly. Here is another comparison in a core values OS perspective:

Feature	Post-Traumatic Stress Disorder (PTSD)	Moral Injury (MI)
Primary Emotion	Fear, Helplessness, Horror	Guilt, Shame, Betrayal, Anger at Self/Others
Source of Trauma	Threat to *physical safety or life* (e.g., I might die)	Threat to *moral identity or conscience* (e.g., I did something wrong, or a trusted authority did something wrong)
Core Value Challenge	Safety, Security, Autonomy	Integrity, Justice, Reverence for Life
Recovery Focus	Reducing fear response (extinction) and regulating the nervous system (polyvagal theory)	Moral repair, self-forgiveness, reconciliation with one's actions, and reconnection to a valued purpose

In simpler terms, a person with PTSD might fear an external threat (a car backfiring), while a person with MI suffers from an internal judgment ("I am unworthy/bad because I failed my moral duty").

The core value operating system is uniquely suited for addressing the spiritual and ethical wounds of moral injury because it forces a shift from shame to reparative action. When MI is triggered, the individual is locked in Option 4 of radical acceptance due to an internal challenge to their Integrity or Reverence for life. The EDT provides a framework for moral repair, with forcing the individual to label the intense shame and guilt, converting it from an overwhelming identity ("I am a bad person") to a diagnosis ("My core values have been challenged by an internal action or witnessed event that is extremely discordant to my beliefs").

The decision to pursue Option 1 (Fix It) or Option 2 (Reframe) constitutes moral repair. This may involve seeking reconciliation, making an honest apology, or engaging in service work that reaffirms the violated value (Litz et al. 2009). The action statement, for instance, *"I affirm my Reverence for Life by volunteering at a veteran's organization,"* is a conscious, sovereign step that replaces paralyzing guilt with restorative action, slowly rebuilding the fracture.

To understand how Option 2 (Changing Perspective) can help heal a moral injury, let's look at the heavy experience of a paramedic working at a mass casualty scene. Imagine this paramedic had to make an impossible triage decision, choosing who to save and who to let die to save as many as possible, and is now struggling to live with that choice.

- **Violated Value:** Reverence for Life or Compassion.
- **Fixing (Option 1) is Impossible:** The event is over; the lives lost cannot be brought back.
- **Change in Perspective (Option 2):** The paramedic shifts the story from *"I am a heartless person who abandoned people who could have been saved"* (Shame) to *"I am a person who bore a heavy burden for the sake of others, and my future must now honour the lives I couldn't save."* Shame is transformed into a lifelong, meaningful Purpose.

The healing happens by turning the event into a duty through a ritual, such as sacred letter writing. The paramedic writes a letter to those who died. This isn't just an apology; it is a deep recognition of their humanity and a promise to carry their memory with honour. The process is finalized with a ritual, like burying the letter in a quiet place or releasing it into a river, symbolizing that the burden has been transformed into a commitment to serve others even better in the future.

The work of moral injury experts like Dr. Melinda J. Keenan emphasizes that healing moral injury requires addressing the deep spiritual and existential core issues, the guilt and shame, that standard trauma treatments often miss (Keenan-Rieker et al. 2018). The process of *moral repair* frequently involves therapeutic interventions grounded in concepts of redemption, forgiveness, and reconciliation.

Back to the conference failure: My mistake was uncontrollable and unfixable. My pain was lingering shame over the violation of Integrity and Discipline.

Option 1: Radical Acceptance (Fix it): I immediately informed the organizers of what happened (a corrective action to restore Integrity). I committed to creating a triple-redundancy check for future presentations (a concrete action to rebuild Discipline). This action repaired the guilt.

Option 2: Radical Acceptance (Change in Perspective). The remaining shame required a shift in perspective. I reframed the problem by:

- **Accepting the experience as a good lesson** in preparation diligence (temporal reframing)
- **Giving myself credit and recognizing I was good at thinking on my feet** in a high-stress situation (value reframing, affirming Temperance and Competence).

The shame dissolved because the internal puppeteer was satisfied: The failure had not been ignored; it had been addressed by corrective action (Option 1) and meaningful reframing (Option 2).

The four options of radical acceptance can also help you with difficult decisions, ensuring that your choices are value-driven. This allows you to vet major decisions against your core values before the stressor hits. For any major internal or external challenge requiring a tough decision, you can analyze it through the lens of Options 1, 2, and 3 of radical acceptance before acting. For example, before taking any drastic action (like quitting a job or confronting a partner), spend at least 24 hours trying to apply Option 1 (Fix) and Option 2 (Change in Perspective). If both fail, Option 3 (remove yourself) becomes an option.

Decision: Should I Change Careers?	**Choice Outcome**	**Affirmed Core Value**
Option 1: Change/ Fix	Negotiate terms, ask for a new role, or train for a new position in the same company.	Growth, Discipline
Option 2: Reframe	Accept the salary for stability, focus on personal projects outside work, and view the job as a temporary lesson.	Security, Patience
Option 3: Remove	Quit immediately to pursue a dream.	Courage, Autonomy

Radical acceptance can also help you repair a relationship damaged by internal failure, yours or your partner's. When you know you did something wrong in your relationship, apologize sincerely and use Option 1 (Fix it — corrective action) to repair your specific violating behaviour (e.g., stop yelling). When your partner does something wrong, try Option 2 (Reframe your Perspective) to accept your partner's flaws as human, viewing the conflict as an opportunity to affirm your own commitment or patience. This may be a hard pill to swallow at first, but we'll get more into it in Chapter 15. If the behaviour is abusive or irreparable, move to Option 3 (Remove Yourself) to affirm your Safety and Self-Respect.

It is important to acknowledge the dark context of Option 3 (Remove Yourself). For some, the ultimate removal from a situation where internal and external pain becomes overwhelming is suicide. When an individual has limited tools to engage their internal locus of control and feels completely fused with the overwhelming pain, they may believe the only remaining option is to be a permanent escape from the self. The entire purpose of the Emotional Diagnostic Tool is to give you the resources to never see this as a viable option.

Here's a scenario to consider that may give you a new perspective on suicide:

You are trapped on the 86th floor of a burning building.

Option 1: Fix It – You can't because the fire is too intense and well beyond the effectiveness of a fire extinguisher. The fire exits are blocked, and there's no escape.

Option 2: Change Your Perspective – This doesn't really apply here, other than coming to terms with how you lived your life and that you are probably going to die.

Option 3: Remove Yourself from the Situation – This is an option almost anyone would understand. This is jumping out the window because it's better than burning to death. This is suicide, but we understand the reasoning. For many who are suffering and die by suicide, their *perspective* may be the choice between jumping (suicide) or burning to death (continuing to suffer).

Option 4: Do Nothing and Suffer – Die a painful death by burning in the fire.

Suicidal ideation may involve the lack of capacity to realize that suicide is a permanent solution to a temporary problem. Prolonged trauma can rob the individual of the ability to recognize the trouble they are in. Crisis intervention is beyond the scope of the EDT and requires the help of a trained professional.

Option 4 of radical acceptance — doing nothing and suffering — is what many unconsciously choose when they lack cognitive distancing in everyday, non-life-threatening situations. Without cognitive distancing, your mind might remain fused with your maladaptive core beliefs, and you become stuck. You simply sit in the suffering, hoping that things will magically get better on their own.

CHAPTER 13

Radical Acceptance for External Challenges

YOU NOW HAVE the complete Emotional Diagnostic Tool (Steps 1–4) at your disposal. This gives you a clear map for repairing your inner peace and a solid strategy for valuing yourself from the inside out, rather than waiting for others to do it for you. In an ideal world, the simple, disciplined application of taking your power back by cutting the puppeteer's string for an external challenge would restore, or at least improve, your internal peace and affirm your emotional sovereignty. However, we do not live in an ideal world.

This chapter addresses the crucial fail-safe protocol: what to do when an external challenge is so painful, so profound, or so repetitive that the shame and fear it triggers overwhelms your cognitive efforts. When even your strongest action statements fail to bring you some peace, the external problem has become an internal issue. The string has been cut, but the pain of the string remains. This is when you deploy the Four Options of Radical Acceptance again, just as when the source of your challenged core value comes from within — but with a few tweaks.

Self-validation means you stop waiting for other people to give you a gold star and start giving one to yourself. Instead of hoping someone else acts right so you can feel good, you choose to feel good because *you* acted right. You do this by making an action statement that proves you are living by your own values. It is a powerful way to change your thinking. However, some hurts are so deep that a quick mindset shift isn't enough to take away the pain.

Profound Violation: The violation is a profound, destabilizing betrayal (e.g., infidelity, financial deceit).

Safety Threat: The external challenge threatens your literal survival or emotional stability (e.g., job loss during a recession).

Traumatic Trigger: The external event hooks directly into an old, unhealed core belief or trauma you have, creating a deep emotional fusion that makes it nearly impossible to get out of.

In these moments, your anger at the external puppeteer (the person or situation challenging your core value) may turn into paralyzing shame and despair within you. You have done the work:

1. **Recognize Upset:** e.g., *I am observing intense, burning despair.*
2. **Identify Value:** e.g., My core values of Trust and Security are challenged.
3. **Identify Source:** e.g., External (My partner broke my trust).
4. **Self-Validate:** e.g., *I validate my Trust by being trustworthy and maintaining my personal integrity. My partner may choose as they wish … but I still feel horrible.*

Validating your core value internally doesn't make you feel any better. This indicates that the external action has caused an internal wound so severe that it requires additional interventions.

The Four Options of Radical Acceptance are a tool for accepting a reality that you cannot control. When you're dealing with the internal challenge (you challenge your own core values), radical acceptance leads to self-correction. When dealing with the profound external challenge (others challenge your values), radical acceptance leads to self-healing and moving forward.

Scenario: After years of marriage, you discover your spouse has been financially deceptive, putting your core value of Trust and Security at grave risk. You have performed the four steps of the Emotional Diagnostic Tool, but the pain is overwhelming and remains. The question then becomes: *Given the external reality that my partner has behaved this way, and I cannot control their past actions, how do I proceed with my life in alignment with my values?*

Path of Acceptance	**Action in the Context of Broken Trust**	**Goal of Self-Validation**
Option 1: Change or Correct the Situation (Fix)	**External Action:** Demand full transparency, immediate therapy, financial protection (new contracts), and proof of change.	**Affirms**: Self-Respect and Accountability. You demand the controllable external fix that allows you to *consider* staying.
Option 2: Reframe or Change the Perspective (Mindset Shift)	**Internal Action:** Accept that trust is broken. Reframe the situation not as the *end* of your life, but as a painful *beginning* to a new life chapter. View the pain as necessary information. Then ask: Can this be a path to understanding and discovering new aspects of your relationship?	**Affirms:** Wisdom and Resilience. The pain is converted into a lesson that guides future boundaries and self-trust.

Option 3: Remove Yourself from the Situation (Escape)	**External Action:** Initiate legal separation or divorce proceedings to sever ties and protect your physical/financial Safety.	**Affirms**: Safety and Sovereignty. You declare that your worth is non-negotiable and requires removing the threat.
Option 4: Do Nothing and Suffer (Paralysis)	Remain in the relationship, secretly resentful, doing nothing to fix the financial instability or emotional damage. The situation festers.	This validates your maladaptive core belief that you are powerless and undeserving of trust or safety.

The most important thing to realize is that when someone or something deeply hurts you, just " thinking differently" isn't always enough. In these cases, radical acceptance means acknowledging that your boundaries have been crossed and that you must take real-world action to heal. Depending on the situation, you have three real-world choices to protect your values:

- **Option 1: Fix it.** If the situation can be repaired, take the physical steps to make it right.
- **Option 2: Reframe and Repair.** If the damage is permanent, do the heavy internal work to find a new purpose for that pain.
- **Option 3: Leave.** If the environment is toxic or dangerous, the only way to honor your self-respect is to walk away physically.

While saying your action statement out loud is a great start, it's only the first step. If the wound to your core values is deep enough, your brain won't feel safe again until you take a physical action to protect yourself.

This process directly addresses the limit of *Self-Empowerment*, the belief that simply knowing your values and maintaining a positive attitude may not be enough to overcome all your suffering. The core value OS acknowledges that we are physically existing in a world of uncontrollable external factors. When a loved one breaks your Trust, the anguish is a deep physiological threat to the structures that ensure survival (security, cooperation). Self-Empowerment fails when it suggests you should simply reframe the betrayal as a "learning experience" while continuing to be exposed to the threat. The Emotional Diagnostic Tool succeeds because it uses pain as a signal that Option 1 is the correct choice. Option 2 may be necessary if the issue is irreparable and safe, and Option 3 may be needed if Options 1 and 2 don't work.

Never *willingly* choose Option 4. Your brain might try to trick you into thinking this is the "easier" path because it feels familiar; this is just your old fears trying to keep things the same. It may feel easier to avoid a hard conversation or a big change right now, but that creates emotional debt you have to pay back later, with interest. Your brain likes to prove its old, negative stories right (e.g., *"See? Things never work out for me"*). Doing nothing gives your brain the evidence it needs to keep you stuck (confirmation bias).

This may be a new way of thinking for you and may even seem counterintuitive. But remember: If you want a change in your life, it's not likely to come to you without effort. You must be willing to act decisively to protect your core values, even if the action is painful. This disciplined practice of diagnosing pain, cutting external strings, and taking radical action has a transformative neurological benefit. It is the final reward for your dedicated effort in the forest of your mind. Recall the concept of neuroplasticity: The repeated firing of a pathway strengthens it, making it the new default pathway that your brain will automatically take.

The core value OS is a muddy path in the forest of your brain. It requires intense concentration (Steps 1-4 of the Emotional Diagnostic Tool). When your neural pathways eventually widen (neurons that fire together wire together), you automatically use cognitive distancing and deploy your action statements with minimal effort. Eventually, your new core value OS becomes the superhighway. Self-validation of your core values becomes automatic, and over time, you will find that you will rely less on the emotional diagnostic tool because you are less bothered by events that triggered you in the past, and the brain rewiring has become complete.

Past Experience (Core Belief OS)	**Future Experience (Core Value OS)**
External Event: A colleague criticizes your report	**External Event:** A colleague criticizes your report
Old Response: Instant fusion with shame, Option 4 (suffer and do nothing) is chosen automatically.	**New Response:** Automatic activation of cognitive distancing, the core value OS fires first.
Internal Experience: Days are spent ruminating on *"I am incompetent,"* feeling paralyzed.	**Internal Experience:** The critical thought is identified as external noise. The action statement is affirmed, leading to immediate focus on controllable fixes (e.g., *How can I improve the next report?*).

The Result: The upset persists because the core belief system has been reinforced.	**The Result:** The upset fails to take hold because the self-worth is validated by the internal value, leaving the brain free to move forward.

The ultimate goal of the EDT is to make its conscious application unnecessary for your routine stressors. The shift happens, not because your world changes but because your internal operating system becomes so robust and efficient that external challenges are automatically categorized as uncontrollable noise, requiring only a swift internal affirmation of self-worth before they are dismissed. The Four Options of Radical Acceptance ensure that even the most destabilizing external betrayals you experience do not destroy you, but instead, they become the catalyst for the strongest, most value-aligned choices of your life. They are the pathway and expression to self-sovereignty.

CHAPTER 14

The Emotional Diagnostic Tool in Action

YOU HAVE NOW completed the entire blueprint for the core value operating system. From defining your values to understanding the neuroscience of emotional fusion and the final protocol of radical acceptance, you possess all the necessary components. This chapter simplifies the complexity into a single, cohesive, four-step tool that you can deploy instantly in the face of any upset. This is where the theory becomes practical, immediate action. This is the Emotional Diagnostic Tool (EDT) in its distilled, usable form.

The Emotional Diagnostic Tool

Step 1: Recognize you're in a bad mood
Step 2: Identify the core value being challenged
Step 3: Determine external or internal validation
Step 4: Use action statement or radical acceptance

- Use action word
- Confirm that your core value is intact internally
- Realize others can feel as they wish without affecting your values

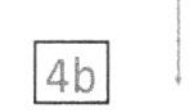

1. Alter or change stressor
2. Learn to live with the stressor
3. Remove yourself from the stressor
4. Do nothing and suffer the consequences

The goal of this simple process is to switch your brain from panic mode to thinking mode in just a few seconds. Instead of letting your emotional center (HPA Axis) run the show, you use your core values and action statements like a manual to put your logical center (dlPFC) back in charge.

Think of it like a manual override for your brain. But before you can reverse engineer a bad feeling, you need your toolkit ready.

Your Top Ten Core Values List: Your list must be easily accessible. Keep a photograph of your Top Ten Core Values as your phone's background or in a dedicated note on your phone. This ensures that when you need to identify the core value being challenged, your critical data is just one tap away, interrupting the brain's default to core beliefs (old, automatic thought patterns). In addition to having your core values accessible on your phone, stick them on your fridge and put them on the mirror in your bathroom so you can access them often, even when you don't need to reverse-engineer a negative experience.

Your Action Statements: Know the specific, controllable action associated with each of your Top Ten Core Values. Verbalizing your 10 core values and action statements often will solidify this mantra in your mind. For many of my clients, I suggest they repeat it to themselves every morning and again before they go to sleep.

The 4 Steps of the EDT

Step 1: Recognize Upset – The Stop and Scan

The first step to feeling better is learning how to catch yourself the moment you get upset. This is the concept of cognitive distancing mentioned in earlier chapters. It is basically a manual override for your nervous system. The goal is to interrupt your brain's alarm bell, the amygdala, before it floods your mind and body with stress hormones and shuts down your ability to think clearly. If you realize that a situation is hitting one of your deep core values and causing a big emotional reaction, use these tools to step back:

- **The Pause:** Stop what you're doing.
- **The Scan (The 5x5 Rule, if needed):** Force yourself to take five deep breaths and then name five objective facts you can observe in your environment (e.g., the color of the wall, the sound of the air conditioning, the texture of the desk). This sensory grounding technique helps disengage the emotional brain before proceeding and bring the forest ranger of your brain (dlPFC) back online.
- **The Label (Name It to Tame It):** Use emotionally neutral language to categorize the feeling and the thought.

"I am observing a strong wave of frustration."
"Ah, there's the old core belief of not being good enough."

Step 2: Identify the core value from your top ten list that is being challenged.

Step 3: Is your core value being challenged externally or internally?

Step 4: Take Action

<u>4A</u>. If the Challenge is External:

The solution is to cut the string using your voice, redirecting your sense of worth inward (Self-Empowerment).

1. **Verbalize Your Action Statement:** State the controllable action you will take to honour your value (e.g., "I validate my Respect by being respectful and maintaining my composure").
2. **State Sovereignty:** Immediately follow with the statement: "And others can do as they wish without challenging my core values" (the "Let Them" theory).
3. **Result:** Peace should return, as your emotional state is detached from the external, out-of-your-control action.

4B. If the Challenge is Internal or the External Protocol Fails:

The solution is radical acceptance: choosing an action that heals the internal wound or accepting the unchangeable reality. Select one of the following four paths:

- **Option 1: Fix It (Change or Correct):** Take immediate, corrective action to repair the violation (e.g., apologize, redo the work, pay the debt). *Affirms Integrity/Discipline.*
- **Option 2: Reframe (Change the Perspective):** Accept the unchangeable reality and consciously apply a perspective shift (temporal or value reframing) to find the lesson or wisdom in the pain. *Affirms Wisdom/Resilience.*
- **Option 3: Remove (Escape the Situation):** Physically terminate your involvement with the source of the pain (e.g., leave the conversation, quit the job, end the relationship). *Affirms Safety/Sovereignty.*
- **Option 4: Do Nothing and Suffer (The Unconscious Default):** *Do not choose this path.*

Simplified Steps	What to Do (The Action)	Why It Works (The Goal)
Step 1: Recognize Upset	**Pause.** Step back and tell yourself, "I am feeling upset right now."	This stops your brain's alarm bell (Amygdala) and tells your inner forest ranger (dlPFC) to take charge.
Step 2: Identify Value	Look at your list of core values and pick the one that feels hurt (e.g., Respect, Honesty).	This turns a messy, "bad" feeling into a specific problem you can actually work with.
Step 3: Identify Source	Ask: "Did I let myself down, or did someone else cross a line?"	This tells you exactly where the problem started and how to best process it.
Step 4: Act and Affirm	Execute the protocol based on the source (internal or external).	This is the final step that repairs your self-worth and proves you live by your own rules.

Let's run three common scenarios with this template.

Scenario 1: The Broken Commitment (External)

The Upset: Your parents constantly criticize your choice of partner. They told you that you're not capable of making decisions on your own, even though you're now an adult with a family of your own.

Step	Action	Dialogue
Step 1: Recognize Upset	If Activated, pause. 5x5 Scan.	"I am observing intense, sharp Anger and the thought of All-or-Nothing Thinking *('They don't trust me,' 'They are terrible parents', I'm not good enough')*."
Step 2: Identify Value	Scan your top 10 core values list.	Challenged value: Trust and Authenticity
Step 3: Identify Source	Analysis.	External. (Your parents' action caused the violation).
Step 4: Act and Affirm	Verbalize Action Statement and Sovereignty.	*"I validate my core value of Trust by being a trustworthy person and by trusting those worthy of my trust. My parents can think what they want without challenging my core values. If they don't trust I know what's best for me, then that's their problem."* *"I validate my core value of Authenticity by living true to my core values and who I am. My parents can think what they want without challenging my core values. They no longer get to define who I am."*
Result	Peace	The power your parents have over you is decreased because your internal sense of trust and authenticity is affirmed by *your own* commitment. You can now decide what to do about it and what barriers you want to put in place for your parents.

Scenario 2: The Self-Violation (Internal)

The Upset: You impulsively max out a credit card on a bedazzled gold frog you see in a shop while travelling (you love frogs), blowing your vacation budget. You feel immense guilt and self-loathing when you get home and unpack.

Step	Action	Dialogue
Step 1: Recognize Upset	Pause. Stop looking at the bedazzled frog.	*"I am observing profound Guilt and Shame, and the thought of Emotional Reasoning ('I feel weak, so I am weak')."*
Step 2: Identify Value	Scan your top 10 core values list.	Violated value: Discipline
Step 3: Identify Source	Analysis	Internal (Your own action caused the violation).
Step 4: Act and Affirm (Radical Acceptance)	Choose Option 1 (Fix) and Option 2 (Reframe).	**Option 1 (Fix):** *"I will immediately return the item or call the credit card company to set up a mandatory payment plan."* **Option 2 (Reframing/Self-Compassion):** *"I accept that I made a mistake, but I affirm my Discipline by using this intense feeling of guilt as motivation to be stricter with my future budget. This single mistake will be the last time."*
Result	Self-Mastery	The self-loathing converts to motivation. You successfully use the mistake to strengthen the value — a lesson learned.

Scenario 3: The Persistent Frustration (External Fail-Safe)

The Upset: You follow all the rules of the road, but someone cuts you off and then gives you the middle finger. You deploy the external protocol for Respect, but the rage and elevated heart rate refuse to subside after a few minutes.

Step	Action	Dialogue
Steps 1–3	Completed. Source is external. The action statement doesn't resolve the bad feelings.	**Initial Action Statement:** "*I validate my Respect by being respectful and remaining courteous.*" **Result:** Heart rate is still high, and you still feel angry. Move to radical acceptance.
Step 4: Act and Affirm (Radical Acceptance)	Choose Option 2 (Reframe) and Option 3 (Remove).	**Option 2 (Reframe):** "*I accept that this driver's road rage is a reflection of their internal chaos, not my worth. I will reframe this as a successful test of my Patience.*" **Option 3 (Remove):** "*I will change lanes and create significant distance between this driver and myself to remove the threat to my Safety and Temperance.*"
Result	Physical Safety and Calm	Once you have physically removed yourself, you can then shift your perspective to help your nervous system calm down and recover. This process might feel difficult and clunky at first, but with practice, your brain will start doing it automatically.

The discipline of consciously applying the EDT over time is your investment in brain learning (neuroplasticity). Your goal is to make the tool redundant for routine stressors. Eventually, when that driver cuts you off, it won't even phase you. Instead, you think, "Wow, must be shitty to be that guy."

Initial attempts may take five minutes of focused effort. When the new neural pathway is established in the forest of your brain, your brain starts to default to cognitive distancing and the internal locus of control.

This is why things that used to ruin your day won't upset you as much anymore. You aren't ignoring what's happening in the real world; instead, you've trained your brain to look at everything through the filter of your own values. The noise of other people's opinions and demands, the things that used to pull your strings like a puppet, fades away. You are left in charge of yourself, feeling calm and at peace.

The EDT can be your lifetime companion. It is the practice of self-empowerment, one conscious choice at a time. The work is never truly done, but the anguish is replaced by purpose, and the victim is replaced by a growth mindset and your sovereign self.

CHAPTER 15

The Ultimate Relationship Tool

IN THIS CHAPTER, we are taking everything you know about your core value operating system and applying it to the most important, and sometimes most painful, part of life: close relationships. Here, the Emotional Diagnostic tool (EDT) shifts from a tool you use to protect yourself to one you use to connect with others, and becomes a map that helps you not only process your own feelings but also understand and bond with your partner.

The pioneering research from the Gottman Institute on thousands of couples has yielded the profound yet comforting statistic that 69 percent of all relationship issues are perpetual (Gottman and Silver 1999). Non-solvable conflicts, which are issues that are perpetual and rooted in fundamental personality differences, needs, or lifestyles, are not indicators of relationship failure. Instead, they represent the inherent, unresolvable friction between two distinct core value and belief operating systems. The goal of your healthy relationship is to manage these issues with respect, understanding, and commitment. It's an opportunity to deepen your understanding of your partner and strengthen your connection. Just because your partner isn't as extroverted as you, it doesn't mean there's something wrong with them. Perhaps you define intimacy differently from your partner. This is likely due to life experiences and observations that were established long before the two of you met. Different doesn't mean wrong; the goal is to understand why your partner feels the way they do, then choose whether to accept the differences and increase your connection or end the relationship.

A common source of these conflicts is unexpressed expectations. We assume our partner values integrity the way we do or that their need for adventure matches ours. When they fail to meet our unexpressed expectations, we face a challenge to our core value, and the anger often leads us to conclude, *"You don't care about me,"* or, *"You're my partner, you should make me happy, and I shouldn't have to tell you how."* The power of the core value OS in a relationship is that it transforms these silent, toxic assumptions into explicit, shared information, providing a cheat sheet to your partner's emotional architecture, revealing what makes them feel great, and what makes them feel horrible. Share your list of core values and your action statements with your partner and have them read this book so they can understand the concepts and share their own core values with you in return.

You may be familiar with Gary Chapman's (2015) Five Love Languages (Words of Affirmation, Acts of Service, Receiving Gifts, Quality Time, and Physical Touch). His framework is invaluable for understanding *how* you and your partner prefer to receive love and feel acknowledged. It also tells you about their sensitivities to how your actions could challenge the love language they identify with.

The core value OS takes Chapman's five love languages to the next level. While love languages tell you *how* your partner likes to receive affection (like gifts or hugs), the core value OS helps you understand *why.* It gives you a deep, diagnostic look at your partner's internal world. Instead of just knowing what they want, you understand the foundational values that make them who they are. Love languages focus on the *delivery* (e.g., "My partner feels loved when I help with the dishes"). By contrast, the core value OS focuses on the *identity* (e.g., "My partner values Reliability; helping with the dishes proves I am a partner they can count on").

Feature	Love Languages	Core Value OS
Focus	Delivery of Affection (Behaviour)	Discover your partner's core values, learning what makes them feel great and what makes them feel bad.
Depth	Focuses on five modes of appreciation	Focuses on ten foundational core values and how your partner expresses them
Why it's Helpful	Shows how your partner receives and expresses love	Explains the *source* of conflict (which value was challenged) and prescribes the action for repair. It also shows you what buttons to push to make your partner feel good.

Knowing your partner's core values allows you to target your love language expression with laser precision, ensuring that the act of service or quality time (love language) is actually stimulating their core values. A powerful exercise you can do with your partner is to sit down together and compare your Top Ten Core Value lists and associated action statements. You may quickly discover where your unsolvable problems lie. You may recognize behaviours or words you've used in the past as challenging their core values without you even knowing it.

Learning each other's core values and action statements opens the door to a deeper understanding of your partner through questioning. The Gottmans call this Love Maps. The more you know your partner, the more you understand why they react and respond to what you do. Ask them about their action statements and why that value is so important to them.

Once the lists are shared, your primary tool for strengthening the bond is deliberate Value Stimulation and Validation.

"How can I stimulate your Core Value of … in our relationship this week?"

Partner's Core Value	Stimulating Action
Respect	*"What can I do to stimulate your core value of respect this week?" "In the past, what did I do to stimulate or challenge that value?"*
Security	*"In what ways do you feel secure? What can I do to help you feel that way?" "Did you feel secure as a child?" "Do you want to talk more about that?" (Love Mapping)*
Growth	*"What does growth mean to you? What have we done as a couple that stimulated that value for you? Have I done anything that challenged that core value for you in the past?"*

This focused approach ensures your efforts are not just appreciated (love language) but that they also nourish your partner's sense of self-worth. When a challenge *does* occur (internal or external), the shared knowledge of your core values allows for empathetic bonding, the act of emotionally connecting over the pain of a challenged value, even if the challenge came from the other person.

The action statement in your partner's ten core values is your relationship cheat sheet. For example, if one of their core values is Authenticity and their action statement for that value is living by their core values, then compliment them when you recognize them living by their values. If one of their values is Trust and their action statement is to be a trustworthy person, acknowledge when that trust is felt and let them know it. It will make them feel great because their core value is being stimulated by you.

The goal is **Understanding, Accepting and Choosing Love Anyway**. This is the relational version of radical acceptance:

- **Understanding:** Acknowledging *why* your partner is in pain. Perhaps their core value of Dependability was instilled because of parents who never did what they said they would. Understanding this sensitivity gives you the knowledge that being dependable matters a lot, and not being dependable will likely hurt more than you realize.
- **Accepting:** Acknowledging the reality of their feelings, even if you disagree with their conclusion. This is accepting your partner for who they are, the good and the bad. Understanding why they take the position they do makes acceptance easier, as in many cases, the true source of the sensitivity has very little to do with you.
- **Choose Love Anyway:** A deeper understanding of what makes your partner tick and knowing the reason they have

> their sensitivities to specific triggers can be invaluable. You may realize that although the energy is directed toward you, the source of the sensitivity may have little to do with you. If both you and your partner choose this mindset, a deeper connection, acceptance, empathetic bonding, and love will be easier to achieve. Choosing love anyway confirms your commitment to each other.

This act of validation is the relational equivalent of cognitive distancing; it separates the problem (the behaviour) from the person (your partner), creating a safe space for repair. I will acknowledge that this is a difficult mindset to achieve, especially when emotions are high. But if you want a positive change in your relationship, then stop doing the things that don't work and try something new.

When you are the external puppeteer and your action challenges your partner's core value (e.g., you broke a promise, violating their Trust), the damage is an internal wound that must be repaired through a validating apology. The repair mechanism for the internal challenge (Option 1 of Radical Acceptance: Fix It) is often a validating four-step apology. Dr. Alison Wood Brooks (2024), the author of *Talk, The Science of Conversations and The Art of Being Ourselves*, has an excellent chapter on how to give effective apologies:

A proper, validating apology must not be about the person apologizing; it must be focused entirely on the wounded party. This means only one problem at a time. Try to resist the urge to say, *"Well, you did this to me, so I don't understand why it's not okay for me to do it to you*!" If it really upset you, put it in your back pocket and bring it up later. If you only want to bring it up when your partner raises an issue, is it really a problem in the first place?

The 4 steps of the Validating Apology

Step 1: Acknowledgment ("I'm Sorry You Feel Bad")

This step requires acknowledging the emotional impact, not just the action.

"I am sorry that you feel bad." The fact is that your partner feels bad. It doesn't matter why, and it doesn't matter if you understand or agree with it.

- **Purpose:** To show you see the pain

Step 2: Validation ("I Can See Why You Feel That Way")

This is understanding your partner's history and sensitivities, as they relate to their challenged core value. This is about putting yourself in their shoes, understanding how they are different, and recognizing that their emotional sensitivities and external stresses are causing them to feel this way.

"I can see why you feel that way. It makes sense to me why you're upset."

- **Purpose:** To show you understand the root of the pain. This is the act of empathetic bonding through understanding.

Step 3: Change ("I'll Do My Best Not to Repeat What I Did")

This is the necessary commitment to Option 1 of the radical acceptance theory (Fix It), a promise of behavioural change.

"I will do my best to ensure this doesn't happen again."

- **Purpose:** To demonstrate that you will make an effort to change.

Step 4: Repair ("What Can I Do Right Now to Make It Better?")

This step gives the power of immediate repair back to your partner.

"Is there anything I can do right now to make this situation better or to make you feel better in this moment?"

- **Purpose:** To initiate the final repair and affirm the partner's Autonomy in their healing process.

Here's a ridiculous scenario I use to illustrate the 4-part apology, showing how these steps can work even in the most bizarre situation: You and your partner are in bed, you've just woken up, and you're about to get ready for your day. You sense your partner is upset.

> ***You:*** *Are you okay? You seem upset.*
>
> ***Your Partner:*** *I'm mad at you.*
>
> ***You:*** *Why? What happened? What did I do?*
>
> ***Your Partner:*** *You kissed my sister … in my dream.*
>
> You giggle, but see that your partner is legitimately upset.
>
> ***Step 1*** – *I can see you're legitimately upset. I'm sorry you feel bad.* Acknowledgement
>
> ***Step 2*** – *I get being mad about a dream. The feelings are legit; I've been there too.* Validation
>
> ***Step 3*** – *In the future, the dream version of me will do better.* Change. (This is a stretch, I know, but if used in this actual situation, it would add some humor and defuse the tension.)
>
> ***Step 4*** – *What can I do right now to make you feel better? Lick your elbows? Suck your toes? Give you a back rub?* Repair

When a validated apology isn't given, then the issue isn't resolved (perpetual). An *"I'm sorry"* followed by a *"but"* isn't sorry at all. Trying to convince your partner they shouldn't be feeling the way they're feeling rarely lands well. It's better to hear them out and let them process and express their emotions.

The Gottman Institute's finding that 69 percent of problems are perpetual leads to a final conclusion: Relationship health is measured not by how often you *agree*, but by how resiliently you *repair* the damage caused by your inevitable disagreements.

If you know your partner's core value is Order, and yours is Flexibility, you can manage the perpetual friction over the laundry or the calendar by deploying the Tool:

1. **Recognize Upset:** *My partner is upset with me.*
2. **Identify their Challenged Value:** Order (challenged by my mess).
3. **Identify Source:** External (My mess is the external stressor to their value of Order).
4. **Act and Affirm (Relational Protocol):** Choose a path of radical acceptance that prioritizes the relationship over the need to be "right."
    - **Option 1 (Fix It):** Fix the mess immediately and affirm their value, even if it feels unfair. You recognize their sensitivity.
    - **Option 2 (Reframe):** Reframe the cleanup not as a chore, but as an act of service that affirms your Commitment to their peace of mind. You recognize your partner's core value of Order was instilled long before you met them.

A central practice promoted by the Gottman Institute for managing perpetual, unsolvable conflict is adopting a unified, detached stance toward the problem, (Gottman and Silver 1999). This concept encourages you and your partner to step outside your emotional reactions and observe the conflict together with curiosity and non-judgment, treating your recurring disagreement as a shared problem rather than a personal flaw of your partner.

- Your partner isn't the problem; it's the stress caused by their job,
- Or the lack of sleep caused by your young kids,
- Or perhaps the fundamental differences you have that were there long before you met.

Unified detachment is basically Step 1 of the EDT (taking a step back) and is done together as a team. Instead of seeing a disagreement as a fight — Me vs. You — you both agree to step back and look at the problem from the outside. You realize the conflict isn't because one of you is a bad person; it's usually a clash between your different core values. The problem (like money or stress) is the issue rather than your partner. You can try to stop attacking each other's character and start working together to fix the real issue.

By taking this detached, shared view, you turn a battle into a project. You accept that you have different operating systems, and your job is to figure out how to make them work together. *The problem is the problem, and together you manage it.*

This approach ensures that your actions are always rooted in conscious value alignment rather than unconscious emotional reaction. The core value OS becomes the shared language that allows two independent, sometimes conflicting, operating systems to coexist harmoniously. This method may seem unintuitive to you and go against your core belief programming, but if you want to improve your relationship, try something different and stop expecting your partner to change to confirm your values. They're not responsible for your happiness.

As Drs. John and Julie Gottman (2018) famously pointed out, there is no such thing as a perfect relationship; there is only a "good enough" one. This doesn't mean settling for less; it means ensuring your core values are being met, while accepting that "bubble collisions" and human imperfections are a natural part of any shared life. Ask yourself, is it more important to be right? Or to be loved?

CHAPTER 16

Trauma, The Body, and The Core Value OS

I WORKED AS an Advanced Care Paramedic and firefighter for twenty years and eventually retired due to a PTSD diagnosis with symptoms that prevented me from doing my job. After receiving support and treatment from a team of mental health professionals, I no longer met the criteria for PTSD. I returned to school and received the education to become a registered counseling therapist specializing in trauma, relationships, and addiction. During that period of reeducation, I analyzed what had happened to me. My traumatized behaviour, emotions, cognitive distorted thinking, relationships, and physical and mental health all began to make sense. "That's why I felt that way," "That's why my relationships suffered." Much of the information in this book is drawn from that experience of post-traumatic growth and recovery, as well as from my specialized training and clinical experience.

It's important to note that a fundamental challenge in trauma recovery is recognizing the difference between *Repair Mode* and *Growth Mode*. When first engaging with the core value OS, an individual recently affected by trauma is often in repair mode, a necessary state of psychological triage where the system's primary goal is simply survival. In this phase, your energy is prioritized for stabilization. This pattern echoes the initial phase of the Triphasic Model of Trauma Recovery established by Judith Herman (1992) and building on the 19th-century work of Pierre Janet (1889). During repair mode, the objective is merely to manage the immediate flood of symptoms and *get safely to tomorrow*; it is often difficult, if not impossible, to build new thought patterns or focus on future-oriented core values like Growth or Purpose. Trying to practice your core values and action statements as a daily mantra when you are just trying to get to tomorrow due to trauma may be too much for your nervous system to handle. Implementing the Emotional Diagnostic Tool (EDT) in the context of trauma needs to be carefully considered in the clinical setting. Only after stabilization is initiated and resources are restored, can you consciously shift to Growth Mode, where your brain has the capacity for the complex neuroplastic work required to solidify your new core value pathways.

The EDT has, until now, primarily functioned as a tool for managing your daily emotional friction. It helps you navigate professional slights, domestic disagreements, and self-inflicted challenges. However, the deepest, most critical application of this entire framework lies in its ability to provide a pathway for healing the wounds inflicted by trauma. This is how I achieved post-traumatic growth from my trauma and how I help my clients do the same … when they are ready to enter the growth mode of their recovery.

Trauma shatters the foundation of core values like Safety, Trust, and Autonomy, replacing them with the paralyzing core beliefs of fear and powerlessness. This chapter will help you bridge what you've learned about the core value OS with the neurobiological reality of what happens to us as a result of trauma.

The work of psychiatrist Dr. Bessel van der Kolk, particularly in his seminal book *The Body Keeps the Score* (2014), revolutionized our understanding of trauma. He demonstrated that trauma is not just a story you tell yourself about the past; it is a physiological event, a sensory, non-verbal memory stored in the most ancient parts of your brain (the limbic system and brainstem). Even your body's musculature and hormonal pathways are affected. When your body is unable to process a threat (e.g., during childhood abuse, combat, or a severe accident), your nervous system may enter a state of persistent defence. Trauma can establish rigid, powerful core beliefs in childhood that operate in direct opposition to your adult core values.

Origin of Belief	The Core Belief	The Challenged Adult Core Value
Childhood Trauma	"I am not safe; I must disappear to survive."	Safety/Autonomy (The right to exist and choose)
Neglect/Abuse	"I am unlovable/ unworthy; my needs are a burden."	Worth/Connection (The belief in inherent value and belonging).
Adulthood Trauma	"The world is fundamentally chaotic and dangerous."	Security/Order (The belief in stability and predictability).

When a person is triggered by a sight, sound, or smell that reminds them of a past trauma, the brain's "alarm system" can take over. It can completely bypass your logical, thinking brain and force your body into fight, flight, or freeze. The problem is that the emotional part of your brain (the limbic system) can't tell the difference between a memory and what is happening right now. It thinks the danger is real and actually happening.

In a brain that has experienced trauma, the pathways between the forest ranger (the logical brain) and the alarm center (the amygdala) can be weakened. This makes it very hard for your forest ranger to send a message to the alarm system saying, "Wait! We are actually safe," which makes it easy for your old core beliefs to jump in and say, "See? I knew the world was a dangerous place." The feeling is intense. Your brain is trying to protect you by reacting fast, but it's using an outdated map. Your body feels like it's in a life-or-death battle, even if you are just sitting in a room thinking of the event or experiencing a smell, vision or location that reminds you of your trauma. This physical reaction makes your negative thoughts feel "proven," even when there is no actual threat.

Trauma can create an internal psychological split, forcing the psyche into defensive roles that operate outside of conscious adult control. This phenomenon is formally described in models such as the Structural Dissociation of the Personality (van der Hart et al., 2006), which suggests that the self divides into survival-oriented parts. To become truly *Unstuck*, we must recognize when our "Adaptive Child" has taken the wheel. As Terry Real (2022) explains in relational life therapy, the adaptive child is the version of us that learned to survive by being right, being loud, or shutting down. But to live a life of peace, we must learn to step into our wise adult, the part of us that can pause, breathe, and choose a response rooted in our core values rather than our old defences.

The wounded child part holds the original, raw pain, fear, and deep shame, the prewired core beliefs established during the trauma, while the adaptive child part develops rigid, protective survival mechanisms, such as hyper-vigilance or emotional shutdown, to manage the overwhelming threat and to protect the wounded child. These defensive states, called "parts" in the Internal Family Systems (IFS) model, represent the automatic, fear-driven operating system that can challenge adult core values like Trust and Autonomy. The ultimate purpose of the core value OS is to bypass these automatic defences and empower the wise adult part of you: the state of conscious self-sovereignty that uses the Emotional Diagnostic Tool to apply value-aligned choices, creating the necessary new pathways in the forest of your brain (neuroplasticity) that override the demands of the wounded and adaptive child versions of you, thereby integrating the trauma and restoring safety. *"I'm no longer a dependent, vulnerable child. I am an independent adult able to defend myself."*

The Emotional Diagnostic Tool's primary function in trauma is to trigger the dlPFC, thinking brain, and restore the adult core value OS, thereby interrupting this primitive defence cascade.

Trauma can rewire how your nervous system handles safety and closeness. This changes your attachment style, which is the blueprint you use to connect with others in your adult relationships. Research by experts like Bowlby and Ainsworth shows that it isn't just trauma that affects you; your early experiences with caregivers also shape these blueprints (Bowlby 1988). These early lessons tell your brain whether people are safe or if getting close to someone is "dangerous." Trauma can keep your body in a state of high alert, making it hard to relax and trust a partner. If your early needs were met, your blueprint says, "Connection is safe." If they weren't (or if you experienced trauma), your blueprint might say, "Connection is risky," leading you to push people away or cling too tightly.

Attachment Style	Self-Image	Image of Others	Interpersonal Relationship
Secure	Positive	Positive	Comfortable with closeness and intimacy
Preoccupied	Negative	Positive	A desire for a high level of closeness with fear of abandonment
Fearful/ avoidant	Negative	Negative	Fear of closeness and socially avoidant
Dismissing/ avoidant	Positive	Negative	Uncomfortable with closeness and overly self-reliant

Trauma can cause the nervous system to perceive intimacy itself as a threat, either of embracement (for the fearful/avoidant style) or abandonment (preoccupied style).

The EDT allows you to diagnose the relational *trigger* instead of fusing with the resulting behaviour:

- **The Trigger:** A partner leaves for a business trip (external challenge to Connection and Security).
- **The Trauma-Response (Core Belief):** Panic and emotional collapse ("They will never come back. I am being abandoned.") Childhood trauma triggered.
- **The Tool's Application:**
    1. **Recognize Upset:** "I am observing intense Fear/ Abandonment and the core belief of absolute loneliness."
    2. **Identify Value:** Security and Worth.
    3. **Identify Source:** External, (the partner's action), but triggered an internal trauma response.

4. **Radical Acceptance (Option 2): Reframe:** "I accept that this feeling of panic is a memory, not a prediction. I validate my Worth by being worthy and honouring the adult reality that I am safe and capable, separate from the trauma memory."

The goal is to provide your conscious adult mind (the core value OS — wise adult) with the resources to override the frightened child's (wounded child) response (the core belief).

Trauma is not limited to childhood.

Individuals often experience uncontrollable anger and shame even outside of actual emergency work environments. The Emotional Diagnostic Tool can provide a structured, sequential, and logical process for managing the chaos of the emotional cascade. My first responder clients like that the Emotional Diagnostic Tool is structured and flows like their protocols or standard operating procedures (SOPs). If "A" happens, then do "B."

For military personnel, police, paramedics, other first responders and public safety personnel, exposure to overwhelming events, often violating their deepest core values of Reverence for Life, Service, Integrity, Safety, and Respect, leads to post-traumatic stress (PTS) or moral injury (discussed in Chapter 12). For these individuals, the constant state of hyper-vigilance (the sympathetic nervous system locked in fight/flight) is a form of survival. The core value OS is helpful by engaging the dlPFC (the reasoning brain) back to the amygdala (the alarm center). This can help confirm safety prior to the body's alarm system being activated.

Step 1 (Cognitive Distancing): The hyper-vigilant mind pauses, stops reacting, and begins observing.

Step 2 (Identify Value): Transforms overwhelming moral injury into manageable information: "My current distress is a profound violation of my Integrity, Respect, etc."

Step 3 (Identify Source, Internal or External): Identify the source of the trauma and remind yourself that you are currently safe. "My memory is activating my body's emergency response, but it isn't actually happening right now; I am safe."

Step 4 (Internal/Fail-Safe Protocol): Allows for the necessary repair, often through Option 2 (reframing cognitive distorted thinking) or Option 1 (corrective action, such as volunteering or speaking out to affirm their Purpose). In this context of trauma, help from a mental health professional is required to implement an intervention to help reconsolidate the experiences (EMDR, Deep Brain Reorienting, Accelerated Resolution Therapy, Reconsolidation of Traumatic Memories or psychedelic therapies).

EMDR is a proven therapy that helps the brain file away traumatic memories properly (Bisson et al. 2013). It works by fixing a specific glitch in how your brain stores traumatic events.

Usually, when something bad happens, your brain processes it and moves it into long-term memory. But trauma gets stuck in your emotional brain (the limbic system) in a raw, frozen state. Because it's not filed correctly, your brain thinks the event is still happening. EMDR fixes this by using bilateral stimulation, which is just a fancy way of saying you move your eyes back and forth, listen to alternating tones, or feel rhythmic tapping while thinking about the memory.

The rhythmic movements force your thinking brain (forest ranger) to stay active and engaged, and finally "talk" to the emotional brain, helping it realize the danger is over so it can process and archive the memory.

The initial act of EMDR (accessing the memory while remaining present and safe) can be an intense form of cognitive distancing because you observe the traumatic content without fusing with it. Reconsolidation of Traumatic Memories (RTM) therapy also does this by having the individual imagine their traumatic experiences playing out as if on a movie screen (Nardo et al. 2018).

To heal from trauma, you need more than just a logical understanding of what happened; you need embodiment, which is the physical ability to feel safe inside your own skin (Levine 1997).

Moving from a trauma reaction back to your values is like moving through the polyvagal ladder we discussed in Chapter 8. You are moving your nervous system from survival mode back to safety mode:

- **The Trauma Default:** When triggered, your body automatically drops you into Dorsal Vagal Collapse (feeling numb or "frozen") or Sympathetic Activation (panic and fight-or-flight).
- **The Action:** When you feel a trigger, use Step 1 (Recognize Upset) and the 5x5 grounding rule (finding 5 things you can see, hear, etc.). This pulls your nervous system back up to the ventral vagal complex, where you feel safe and connected.
- **The Final Affirmation:** In Step 4, when you say your action statement out loud, you are taking your power back. You are telling your primitive brain: "*I am in control now, and I am*

> *safe."* This is your wise adult self stepping in to protect the wounded child part of you.

The goal is to reach a point where you can remember the traumatic event as a fact of your history without your body's "emergency alarm" going off. You keep your peace, even when the memory arises.

I want to be clear that the EDT will *not* be enough to manage severe symptoms from trauma. The core value OS is also *not* a cure for trauma, but it can be a stabilizing mechanism that allows you to safely encounter your triggers, diagnose the source of your pain, and choose a path of value-aligned action (Options 1, 2, or 3 of radical acceptance) rather than falling into the passive paralysis of Option 4. It is the structure that helps your body feel safe by building new, adaptive thought patterns. It is essential to state that anyone suffering from the symptoms of trauma should seek help from a therapist with specialized training in this area.

CHAPTER 17

The Emotional Diagnostic Tool for Anxiety and Depression

THE JOURNEY THROUGH the core value operating system has been about bringing structure to your emotional chaos. This chapter confronts two of the most pervasive and debilitating emotional states of modern life: anxiety and depression. While the Emotional Diagnostic Tool (EDT) is not a substitute for professional medical treatment, it *can* be a cognitive anchor that empowers you to interrupt the self-perpetuating cycles of worry and despair.

Historically, anxiety and depression were viewed as distinct conditions. However, modern clinical research consistently suggests they are often two sides of the same underlying imbalance in emotional regulation (Mineka et al. 1998). Anxiety, particularly Generalized Anxiety Disorder (GAD), is fundamentally a time-travelling mind, characterized by excessive thought focused on what might happen in the future, projecting catastrophic scenarios onto uncontrollable external events (fear of future challenge) (Borkovec et al. 2004). Depression may be caused by your mind being fixated on the past — rumination, regret, and the inability to escape the negative narrative of what already happened (Nolen-Hoeksema 1998).

Both states can hijack your mind, pulling you out of the present moment (the only place where agency exists) and leaving you with a profound sense of helplessness and feelings of inability to change. By forcing your mind to focus on a present, controllable action statement, the EDT provides the cognitive bridge back to the now. Anxiety and depression can be fueled by the belief that you are powerless to change your circumstances. They represent the ultimate triumph of the maladaptive core beliefs ("I am unsafe," "I am unworthy") over the core values. The core value OS is ideally suited as a self-empowerment exercise because it can provide you with a preapproved script for action that is always available, regardless of external circumstances. When your anxious mind throws an uncontrollable scenario at you, the answer is a core value action statement. When the depressive mind sinks into a past regret, the solution is a corrective action statement.

When you feel anxious about failing a presentation, your brain is actually sounding an alarm; your value of Excellence or Competence is likely threatened. Instead of letting that worry spin, you can use a specific action statement to get back on track. This moves your energy away from useless worrying and puts it into productive effort.

When you feel depressed after saying something hurtful to your partner, you may be experiencing a conflict with your internal value of Integrity. Rather than getting stuck in a loop of regret, you can use an action statement or a path of radical acceptance to move forward. This forces your mind to switch from passive overthinking to active self-repair.

We see the power of anchoring oneself to intrinsic values in the lives of many highly successful individuals who navigate intense public pressure, which often triggers severe anxiety and depression. Consider the journey of actress, singer, and entrepreneur Selena Gomez. She has been consistently open about her struggles with anxiety, depression, and bipolar disorder, often detailing the paralysis that comes with public scrutiny and mental health crises. In her public discussions and documentaries, Gomez describes finding stability, not through external validation but by committing to specific, intentional actions, a direct parallel to the core value OS.

Anxiety is an energy management problem: You are spending current energy on a future event you cannot control. The EDT is used to redirect that energy to a controllable, present task.

Example: The Anxiety of Financial Ruin (Core Value: Security)

The Anxious Thought: "I might lose my job next month, and if I do, I will lose my home and become bankrupt. I worry about this constantly."

EDT Step	Action	Dialogue (Internal Action Statement)
Step 1: Recognize Upset	Pause. 5x5 Scan: name five things (if your anxiety is causing physical activation).	"I am observing intense, escalating Fear and the thought of Catastrophizing."
Step 2: Identify Value	Scan your top 10 core values list.	Challenged value: Security (Action Statement: *I practice my core value of financial security by committing to responsible management of my resources*).

Step 3: Identify Source	Analysis	External, (the threat of job loss).
Step 4: Act and Affirm (External Protocol)	Verbalize Action Statement and Sovereignty	"I'm going to validate my Security by updating my resume, reviewing my budget, and saving money today … and others can do as they wish (the economy can fluctuate) without challenging my core values. I'll adapt as needed."
Result	Potential peace from taking action	The worry about the *future* is diminished by a sensible, present-day action statement, placing a sense of control in your own hands and taking action you can implement now. The anxiety loop is broken because you realize what's in your control and what is not.

If the anxiety persists, you move to the fail-safe protocol (radical acceptance): Option 2 (Reframe) is often the best choice for anxiety, acknowledging the fear but reframing the potential worst-case scenario as something the wise adult part of you is capable of handling.

Depression may be an action management problem: You may be immobilized by an internal narrative of worthlessness derived from the past. The EDT is used to force movement and repair.

Example: The Depression of Past Regret (Core Value: Integrity)

The Depressive Thought: "I regret how I treated my trusted friend. I am a bad person, and I can never fix it."

EDT Step	Action	Dialogue (Internal Action Statement)
Step 1: Recognize Upset	Pause. Deep breath.	"I am observing heavy Sadness/Guilt and the thought of Personalization" ("I am a bad person").
Step 2: Identify Value	Scan your top 10 core values list.	Violated value: Integrity (Action Statement: *I practice my core value of Integrity by living in alignment with my word and my truth*).
Step 3: Identify Source	Is this something I did or someone else?	Internal, (my past action caused the violation). Move to radical acceptance.
Step 4: Act and Affirm (Internal Protocol)	Choose Option 1 (Fix) and Option 2 (Reframe).	**Option 1 (Fix):** "I will immediately text or call my friend, or write a letter, offering a sincere, validating apology using the 4-part apology from Chapter 16 for my past actions, affirming my current Integrity." **Option 2 (Reframe/Self-Compassion):** "I accept that I was a less integrated person five years ago, but I validate my Growth by making amends today, demonstrating that my value of Integrity is now paramount."
Result	Potential release of guilt and energy	The shame over the *past* dissolves into a present-day **Option 1 (Fix)**, which can mobilize the depressed energy and restore a sense of agency and worth.

- Anxiety attempts to pull you into an uncontrollable future.
- Depression attempts to glue you to an unchangeable past.

The core value OS can be a constant, reliable anchor that snaps your focus back to the only moment where you have power: the present.

The process of using the EDT is, fundamentally, a structured, applied mindfulness practice. It turns the abstract concept of "being present" into a tangible, four-step exercise, helping you achieve and sustain the present moment.

EDT Step	Mindfulness Principle Applied	Why It Works
Step 1: Recognize Upset	**Non-Judgmental Awareness.** You pause and label the feeling ("I am observing fear") without immediately attaching a judgment ("This fear means I am weak").	This is the instant creation of the present moment, the only moment where observation is possible.
Step 2: Identify Value	**Targeted Attention.** You focus your awareness away from the emotion's chaos and onto your preapproved core values list.	You shift attention from the past/future narrative to the present, objective data (the value list).
Step 3: Identify Source	**Acceptance of Reality.** You accept the reality of the situation (Is it *my* fault or an *external* factor?) without demanding that the reality be different.	You pave the way for a non-reactive response.
Step 4: Act and Affirm	**Intentional Action.** You choose a specific, present-day behaviour (your action statement) to affirm your value, replacing rumination or worry with present-time affirmations.	You anchor yourself to the *now* by performing a controllable action, shutting down the time-travelling mind.

By using the Emotional Diagnostic Tool over and over again, you are doing much more than just getting by. You are actually building new pathways in your brain that allow your calm, wise-adult self to stay in charge and remain confident in your own worth. Taking intentional actions aligned with your values is a reliable way to empower yourself. Eventually, this leads to a natural state of mindfulness in which stressful thoughts about the past or future are less likely to control you.

I want to stress again that the EDT isn't the magic cure to severe mental health issues like PTSD, anxiety, and depression. I urge you to seek help from a mental health professional when you are having difficulty navigating the symptoms of these serious conditions.

CHAPTER 18

Why Peace is a Better Destination

FINDING INNER PEACE is the potential reward of implementing the exercises in this book and it's important to distinguish peace from happiness. The cultural programming of the modern world champions the pursuit of happiness. From self-help gurus to advertising campaigns, you are constantly sold the idea that life's ultimate goal is a state of perpetual joy, pleasure, and excitement. Yet, the relentless chase for this fleeting emotion can be a source of your deep anxiety and dissatisfaction. This chapter argues that the true, sustainable aim for a fulfilled life is inner peace: the resilient foundation rooted in your self-sovereignty, a stable internal state from which all your positive emotions, including happiness, can authentically arise.

I want you to understand that the inner peace we are talking about isn't just a feel-good concept I'm pitching to you. It is a measurable psychological state rooted in how you use your values.

In 2004, two psychologists, Christopher Peterson and Martin Seligman, set out to map the best parts of human nature. They led a massive, three-year project involving over 50 scientists to examine what has historically made humans resilient across 2,500 years of culture and philosophy. The result was the Values in Action (VIA) classification (Peterson and Seligman 2004).

What they discovered is significant for you and your journey toward peace. They found that when you identify and live through your most authentic core values, you create a psychological buffer. This isn't about being happy all the time; it's about having a sense of meaning and stability that happiness alone can't provide.

Think of it this way: Happiness is like a sunny day; it's great while it lasts, but you can't control the weather. Inner peace, supported by your values, is like having a well-built, sturdy home. Even when the storm of a "bubble collision," — opposing domains of core beliefs — hits or life gets chaotic, your foundation doesn't shake.

The research shows that people who align their daily actions with their core values report significantly lower stress and higher life satisfaction (Peterson and Seligman 2004). In my work as a therapist and in my years as a first responder, I've seen this play out in real time.

When you stop chasing the high of happiness and start building the bedrock of your values, you aren't just surviving the day; you are becoming unshakable. You are choosing a destination that stays with you long after the fleeting moments of happiness have faded.

One of my partners on the ambulance was an amazing medic with decades of experience. He was always happy, and the stress around our work environment never seemed to faze him. He never engaged in "shop talk" and never spoke poorly of anyone we worked with. One day I commented on how I noticed his consistent positive attitude. He told me that when he comes to work, his focus is being a good medic and firefighter based on his values and definitions of professionalism. If he tried to satisfy everyone else's expectations, he would have quit long ago.

The core flaw in pursuing happiness is that, by definition, it is a fleeting emotional state that often depends on external circumstances, such as others pleasing you. Psychologists frequently refer to the hedonic treadmill, a concept demonstrating how you quickly return to a relatively stable level of happiness despite major positive or negative events:

1. **Positive Event:** You receive a promotion, buy a new car, or fall in love.
2. **Happiness Spike:** Your mood soars; you believe this new state will last forever.
3. **Adaptation:** Your brain habituates to the new stimulus, and the new normal is established (Domjan 2015). The excitement fades, and you seek the *next* external event to trigger another spike.

My bulldog, and many other dogs — maybe yours if you have one — are excellent examples displaying the hedonic treadmill. When I tell Dexter, "Uncle Steve is coming over!" he jumps on the sofa, licks my face, wiggles his bum, then runs to the door and sits there, waiting for my friend Steve to arrive, the positive event. When he arrives, Dexter will run out to greet him, expressing overwhelming joy and happiness, the happiness spike. Ten minutes later, he's sleeping on his bed while Steve and I watch the hockey game (go Oilers), the adaptation, Dexter's new normal. I think cats also experience the hedonic treadmill; they likely just act way cooler about it.

In contrast to happiness, peace is an internal state of non-resistance to the present moment. It is your conscious decision to accept reality as it is, without demanding it conform to your preferences. Peace is the solid foundation you build when your life is guided by a clear set of personal rules and principles. Instead of feeling uncertain, you feel steady because you know exactly what you stand for. True peace is the constant feeling you get when your life is built on a solid foundation of clear, personal principles. When you know exactly what you stand for, you create an internal strength that doesn't shake, even when things get difficult. It is your quiet confidence that, even when external events threaten your safety, your internal core values remain intact.

- It is your realization that your Worth is inherent, not conditional upon external approval or success.
- It is your psychological immunity achieved when the wise adult overrides the demands of your automatic, fear-based responses.

You may want to change your relationship because you no longer feel happy in it or wish to be the rolling stone that gathers no moss because you get bored easily. You can move, change, escape, and try new things in the pursuit of happiness on the hedonic treadmill, but the truth is, no matter where you go, run, or travel … there you are. Strive to be the 2.0 version of yourself, the wise-adult version of you, and use your list of core values as a guide to achieve the new you.

As the Dalai Lama teaches, "Peace does not mean to be in a place where there is no noise, trouble, or hard work. It means to be in the midst of those things and still be calm in your heart" (Dalai Lama XIV 1999). Peace, unlike happiness, is a sustainable state because it is built from the inside out, making it the most resilient pursuit for long-term well-being.

The distinction between fleeting happiness and enduring peace is a central pillar of Eastern philosophy, particularly in Buddhism. Buddhist teachings hold that life is characterized by *dukkha* (often translated as suffering, dissatisfaction, or unease), which arises from attachment and craving (Rahula 1974). This craving for specific outcomes, such as the desire for perpetual happiness, is seen as the root of suffering.

The Attachment: You attach your internal worth to the condition of being happy.

The Change: The external condition that created happiness (e.g., a perfect vacation, a successful project) inevitably changes or ends.

The Suffering: Because you were attached to the condition, the change causes distress, disappointment, and an immediate search for the next fix.

The philosopher Alan Watts (who heavily synthesized Eastern philosophy for a Western audience) summarized this pursuit by saying, "Trying to manage things, trying to force things to conform to your will … You just wear yourself out" (1975). Buddhism offers non-attachment as the path to peace. Non-attachment is your conscious decision to engage fully with life's joys and sorrows without allowing your internal stability to depend on them.

- **Acknowledge Impermanence:** Try to train yourself to observe feelings of upset without judging them or wishing them away. Accept that the emotion, like all things, will pass. This is the act of being present and creating the necessary space for peace.

- **Practice Non-Control:** Release the need to control the uncontrollable external world (the principle of "Let Them") (Robbins 2024). Detach your internal stability from the outcomes dictated by others or by fate. The Dalai Lama reminds us, "We can never obtain peace in the outer world until we make peace with ourselves."
- **Radical Acceptance:** When faced with a setback or failure, choose to accept the reality of the situation, reframing it as information or a lesson rather than a personal tragedy, thereby detaching your ego and sense of worth from the failure.

When you consistently choose intentional, principle-based action (core values), you practice detaching your core identity from the volatile conditions of external success or failure. When peace is established, happiness becomes a welcome, natural *visitor* rather than an elusive, demanded *master.*

Research in positive psychology shows that you need a steady inner foundation before you can genuinely feel happy for a long time. Studies on self-compassion, which is basically being kind to yourself when things go wrong, show that accepting your struggles without judging yourself leads to less anxiety and more balanced moods (Neff 2003).

Research on the "paradox of happiness" shows that the deliberate pursuit of happiness often backfires, leading to a state of "stuckness" in which the individual becomes hyper-focused on their own lack of fulfillment. Research by Mauss et al. (2011) found that the more people value happiness, the more likely they are to feel disappointed. When we set "being happy" as a goal, we inadvertently monitor our current state for any signs of unhappiness.

This inner stability, or peace, acts like a container for your life. When you aren't constantly overwhelmed by stress or self-criticism, you finally have the space to fully feel and enjoy positive emotions when they happen. Happiness is like a cat. If you chase it, it will run away. If you sit still and do your own thing, it will eventually come to you.

State of Being	Primary Locus of Control	Core Relationship to Emotion
Chasing Happiness	External	Dependence (Requires a continuous stream of positive input).
Achieving Peace	Internal (core values)	Resilience (Is stable regardless of external events).

When you operate from a place of deep, foundational serenity, you are less reactive to stress, forgive failures faster, and navigate relationship friction more effectively. When you feel genuine joy or connection — a perfect campfire (without the bear), a meaningful conversation, or a successful project — you are fully present to receive and appreciate it, precisely because you are not frantically searching for it. As the Dalai Lama beautifully states, "If you want others to be happy, practice compassion. If you want to be happy, practice compassion." The internal path to peace (compassion, self-control) is a reliable generator of genuine happiness.

The highest goal of your new internal operating system, leading to self-empowerment and abundance, is peace through the shift from chasing to anchoring. When your core values are operational, you live a life of profound internal alignment.

Self-Empowerment means you don't feel the need to brag about your accomplishments, show off your new bling, or compete with your neighbours to "one-up" them because the requirement of external validation is no longer there. This state is peaceful, purposeful, and intrinsically motivated. Abundance is your quiet confidence that you possess everything you need to act on your values, regardless of external circumstances. You're self-validating and filling your tank until it overflows. This is a state of psychological sufficiency, true peace. Abundance allows you to give the overflow you're producing to others without the need for reciprocation.

Happiness is fleeting and temporary.

Your happiness will come and go, but peace changes your relationship to whatever comes and goes.

Your peace will allow your happiness, but happiness doesn't guarantee your peace.

Happiness asks, "How do you feel right now?" Peace asks, "How free are you, even when you don't feel good?"

CHAPTER 19

The Path to Abundance

YOU HAVE REACHED the final chapter of the core value operating system journey. This is not an ending, but a profound new beginning. You have moved from unconsciously driven core beliefs to consciously chosen core values. You have exchanged emotional chaos for cognitive clarity.

This final chapter synthesizes the entire framework, focusing on the ultimate reward: The automatic, neurologically wired life of abundance and self-empowerment.

Mother Teresa is perhaps the most radical example of how mental abundance has absolutely nothing to do with what's in your wallet and everything to do with what's in your soul. Think about the "bubble" she lived in. She spent her days in the literal gutters of Calcutta, surrounded by the kind of suffering, disease, and death that would cause most people's nervous systems to shut down completely. Yet, when you see footage of her, you don't see someone who is reactive, frantic, or depleted. You see someone operating from a state of total mental surplus.

Mother Teresa said, "If you are humble, nothing will touch you, neither praise nor disgrace, because you know what you are" (Mother

Teresa 1996). When Mother Teresa spoke of humility, she ultimately referred to radical self-awareness. In clinical terms, this is the ultimate goal of value-alignment: to reach a state where your internal knowing is louder than the external noise. When you know what you are, and more importantly, who you are and what you stand for, you become bulletproof to the praise and the disgrace of the world.

Mother Teresa faced incredible bubble collisions. She was constantly pressured by politicians, scrutinized by the global media, and even criticized by those who didn't understand her mission. But she didn't waste her energy trying to win those arguments or defend her ego. She was so anchored in her core values — compassion, dignity, and service — that the noise of the world couldn't reach her. *She had already decided who she was, so the world didn't get a vote.*

That is the "extra" I'm talking about. She had so much internal peace that she could walk into a room of world leaders and speak her truth without shaking, and then walk into a slum and hold the hand of a dying stranger with total presence. She was giving from an overflow. Mother Teresa showed us that when your life is perfectly aligned with your values, you become an infinite resource. You don't get tapped out by stress because you aren't fighting the world anymore; you are simply being yourself in the middle of it. If she could find a state of abundance while living in poverty and amid conflict, it proves you can find it in your office, your home, or your community. It's not about changing your surroundings; it's about changing the foundation you stand on.

Throughout this book, we have focused on the logical steps of the Emotional Diagnostic Tool (EDT). We have talked about how your forest ranger (the rational part of your brain) can take control of your alarm center (the amygdala) to make a wise choice based on your values. However, before any of those logical steps can work, you have to do the most challenging and scariest thing in your emotional life: be vulnerable. This means being honest about your feelings and admitting when you are hurt, even when it feels messy or terrifying.

Vulnerability is the raw, necessary courage required to show up and be seen, particularly when the stakes are high or the outcome is uncertain. Deploying the EDT is, at its core, an act of vulnerability because it forces you to drop your emotional defences and honestly face the feeling that your self-worth has been challenged.

Positive Toxicity: This is sweeping your problems under the rug because you either don't have the capacity to face them right now, or you lack the vulnerability to face your issues authentically. Eventually, you may trip over that rug, and your body will force you to face your problems. I was a toxic positivist for decades. My body forced me to face the realities of what was happening by altering the effectiveness of my memories and inflicting pain in my bones and muscles.

Tragic Optimism: This is being authentic in evaluating your circumstances, acknowledging the tragedies and giving them the attention they need so you can put them behind you while still maintaining an optimistic mindset. If you face your fears, you may find they are not as scary as you thought. This takes vulnerability.

I can honestly say that all the success I have received as an artist (DanSun) has come from creating authentically from a vulnerable mindset. I don't censor my art or think of how others will react, and the truth is, the more vulnerable and authentic I am in all parts of my life, the more I connect with others.

The world-renowned research of Dr. Brené Brown (2010) on vulnerability and shame provides the perfect framework for understanding why deploying the EDT may be so difficult. Shame is the intensely painful feeling or experience of believing that we are flawed and therefore unworthy of love and belonging. Shame is the quiet, internal voice that whispers, "*You are bad because you feel this way,*" or, "*If others knew you were struggling, they would reject you.*" Shame is the ultimate enemy of the core value OS because its sole function is to prevent Step 1 (Recognize Upset) from happening.

Shame Response	**Why it blocks the EDT**
Hiding/Silence	Prevents **Step 1 (Recognition)**. If you don't admit to the feeling, you can't label it. Toxic Positivity.
Armor/ Defensiveness	Prevents **Step 3 (Identifying Source)**. If you are busy blaming others or circumstances, you cannot honestly diagnose the internal vs. external challenge.
Numbing/Fusing	Prevents **Step 2 (Identifying Value)**. Shame is overwhelming and keeps the system locked in survival, blocking access to the rational core values list.

Shame forces you to fuse with the feeling, making you believe the emotion *is* your identity: *I am a failure* (fusion), rather than *I am observing a feeling of inadequacy* (cognitive distancing). According to Brown, the antidote to shame is vulnerability, which she defines as being "uncertainty, risk, and emotional exposure" (Brown 2012).

To the core value OS:

- **Uncertainty:** Acknowledging that deploying the EDT might lead to an uncomfortable realization (e.g., admitting *you* were the one who violated your Integrity).

- **Risk:** The risk that if you identify your pain, you might have to take a hard, corrective action (Option 1: Fix It) or accept a difficult truth (Option 2: Reframe).
- **Emotional Exposure:** The willingness to feel the sharp, raw sensation of the challenged value without immediately reaching for distraction or defence.

Pain + the unwillingness to face pain = Trauma

Pain + the willingness to face pain (this takes vulnerability) = Growth

The first, quiet act of vulnerability is the internal commitment to observe the pain without judgment. It's the moment you say: "Yes, I am upset. Yes, I am afraid my Worth has been challenged. And I am willing to look at it." This internal consent is the ignition switch for Step 1 of the EDT: Recognize Upset. The need for courage doesn't end after Step 1; it continues through the entire diagnostic and action phase. I get it's tough to authentically do a deep dive on ourselves, but as one of my professors in college told us, "That's where all the juicy bits are."

When you look at your core value list during a crisis, you are confronting the person you *want* to be with the reality of who you *are* at that moment, which can trigger shame. If your value is Temperance, and you just screamed at your children, the shame says, "You are a terrible parent." The EDT forces you to accept: "I violated my value of Temperance, but that failure doesn't define who I am." You vulnerably accept the behavioural lapse while protecting your core identity.

The final, most intense act of vulnerability is often the corrective action. It takes deep vulnerability to look at your partner who is failing you and choose to affirm your own Sovereignty ("I will affirm my Respect by walking away"), rather than fighting to control them and accepting the uncertainty of their continued behaviour.

Apologizing, admitting a mistake, or returning a luxury purchase requires immense vulnerability because you are exposing your error. However, this is the very act that affirms your Integrity and builds resilience. Courageous vulnerability is the pathway to abundance.

Brown defines shame resilience as the ability to move through shame quickly while maintaining a connection to self-worth (Brown 2007). The core value OS is a structured program for building this resilience that shame attempts to hide. The EDT's Step 1, recognize your upset, forces exposure of what you're feeling and labeling that emotion (e.g., "I am feeling shame because I violated my value"). The EDT replaces your harsh self-criticism with the objective, non-judgmental language of your core values by practicing self-compassion and affirming that the mistake is not your identity. The commitment to repair (Fix It) or reframe forces movement out of isolation, the ultimate goal of shame resilience.

Ultimately, mastering the EDT requires the courage to remain vulnerable to your own true feelings. When you choose vulnerability, you choose connection to your feelings, your values, and ultimately, your whole, imperfect, worthy self. Once people close to you see that you are being vulnerable, they are given permission to be vulnerable with you as well. This can increase connection. Our default is, "I will be vulnerable with you once I feel safe to do so," or, "I'll trust you once you show me you're trustworthy." Be vulnerable and trustworthy first, and you will see how it attracts those attributes in others close to you.

This book is designed to help you realize that you have the power to control how you respond to life. Success with this system doesn't mean your problems disappear; it means you get much better and faster at bouncing back when things go wrong. Every time you use the EDT, you are changing your brain. You are choosing to skip the old path that triggers your internal alarm, and instead, build a new, logical path that aligns with your core values to help you make good decisions. The goal of practicing this is to build a shield against overreacting. You want to make this new way of thinking so strong and fast that it becomes your automatic response. Think of it like clearing a new trail in the thick forest of your brain. Eventually, the new path becomes so much easier to walk on that your brain stops using the old, unhelpful trails entirely.

The first few dozen times you use the EDT, it feels like heavy lifting. You have to physically pause, scan your phone for your values, and force the action statement. This is the wise adult battling the entrenched core beliefs and treading a new pathway through the thick brush in the forest of your brain. With repetition, the pathway strengthens. Eventually, the moment a trigger hits you, you will instinctively take a deep breath (Step 1), and the action statement will pop into your mind without effort.

True neurological change to form new habits doesn't happen overnight; it requires a disciplined 63-day cycle to move a new response from a conscious effort to an automated habit with neurobiological changes being felt on days seven, fourteen, twenty-one, forty-two, and sixty-three (Leaf 2021). When this happens, the new wiring is automatic and complete. Situations that shook you in the past — a critical email, a slight from a relative, or someone cutting you off in traffic — simply don't bother you anymore. The external noise is instantly categorized as uncontrollable, and your system automatically affirms your sovereignty. Your window of tolerance widens, resulting in fewer activations from the world's chaos. You are protected, not because the world stopped throwing darts but because you moved your sense of worth out of the target zone. Eventually, you won't feel the need to use the EDT at all because you're no longer being derailed like you used to be.

The concept of self-actualization, popularized by Abraham Maslow, describes the realization of one's full potential and the complete inner peace that comes from living in alignment with your authentic self. The core value OS is a direct operational path to this state. Sustainable abundance is the byproduct of living in constant alignment with your core values. When you are aligned:

Decisions become easy: Choices are filtered through your core value list, eliminating the anxiety of indecision.

Energy is conserved: You stop spending vital energy fighting external battles and internal shame.

Action is purposeful: Every step, dictated by an action statement, moves you toward your deepest sense of Purpose and Growth.

When you live in a way that aligns with your deepest values, you naturally develop a sense of honesty and a clear purpose that others find attractive. People and opportunities are drawn to this kind of consistency because you aren't fighting yourself anymore. When your inner beliefs and outer actions finally line up, life starts to feel smoother, and peace becomes your natural state.

The journey is now in your hands. To maintain and strengthen your core value OS, commit to:

1. **Daily Review:** Spend 60 seconds each morning reviewing your Top Ten Core Values and action statements. This primes the executive decision-making part of your brain for the day's challenges.
2. **Immediate Deployment:** Commit to using the EDT (all four steps) immediately upon sensing *any* upset, no matter how small.
3. **Regular Audit:** Revisit your core value list every six months. Does growth mean something different to you now? Do your action statements still feel potent? Adjust as necessary, knowing that growth is a process of constant recalibration.

You are no longer a passive passenger in your emotional life. You are the architect of your destiny, the master of your mind, and the sovereign ruler of your emotional landscape.

REFERENCES

Aurelius, M., & Hays, G. (2026). *Meditations: A new translation Marcus Aurelius; Gregory Hays*. Pandora's Box.

Beck, A. T., Rush, A. J., Shaw, B. F., Emery, G., DeRubeis, R. J., Hollon, S. D., & Clark, D. M. (2024). *Cognitive therapy of depression*. Guilford Publications.

Bisson, J. I., Roberts, N. P., Andrew, M., Cooper, R., & Lewis, C. (2013). *Psychological therapies for chronic post-traumatic stress disorder (PTSD) in adults. Cochrane Database of Systematic Reviews, 2015*(8).

Borkovec, T. D., Alcaine, O., & Behar, E. (2004). Avoidance theory of worry and generalized anxiety disorder. In R. G. Heimberg, C. L. Turk, & D. S. Mennin (Eds.), *Generalized anxiety disorder: Advances in research and practice*, 77–108. Guilford Press.

Bowlby, J. (1988). *A secure base: Parent-child attachment and healthy human development*. Basic Books.

Brooks, A. W. (2024). *Talk: The science of conversation and the art of being ourselves*. Penguin Press.

Brown, B. (2007). *I thought it was just me (but it isn't): Telling the truth about perfectionism, inadequacy, and power*. Avery.

Brown, B. (2010). *The gifts of imperfection: Let go of who you think you're supposed to be and embrace who you are*. Hazelden Publishing.

Brown, B. (2012). *Daring greatly: How the courage to be vulnerable transforms the way we live, love, parent, and lead*. Avery.

Byrne, R. (2006). *The secret.* Atria Books

Chapman, G. D. (2015). *The 5 love languages: The secret to love that lasts.* Northfield Publishing.

Crum, A. J. & Langer, E. J. (2007). *Mind-set matters: Exercise and the placebo effect. Psychological Science, 18*(2), 165–171.

Crum, A. J., Salovey, P., & Achor, S. (2013). *Rethinking stress: The role of mindsets in determining the stress response.* Journal of Personality and Social Psychology, *104*(4), 716–733.

Dalai Lama XIV. (1999). *Ethics for the new millennium.* Riverhead Books.

Domjan, M. (2015). *The principles of learning and behavior* (7th ed.). Cengage Learning.

Fledderus, M., Oude Voshaar, R. C., Bohlmeijer, E. T., & Pieterse, M. E. (2013). *The relationship between psychological flexibility and cardiac vagal tone: A possible link between ACT and physical health.* International Journal of Behavioral Medicine, *20*(4), 518–525.

Frankl, V. E. (2006). *Man's search for meaning.* Beacon Press.

Goleman, D. (1995). *Emotional intelligence: Why it can matter more than IQ.* Bantam Books.

Gottman, J. M. & Silver, N. (1999). *The seven principles for making marriage work.* Harmony Books.

Gottman, J. M., & Gottman, J. S. (2018, July 18). *The truth about expectations in relationships.* The Gottman Institute.

Häuser, W., Hansen, E., & Enck, P. (2012). *The nocebo phenomenon in medicine: Mechanisms and clinical implications.* Deutsches Ärzteblatt International, 109(26), 459–465.

Hayes, S. C., Strosahl, K. D., & Wilson, K. G. (1999). *Acceptance and Commitment Therapy: An experiential approach to behavior change.* Guilford Press.

Hebb, D. O. (1949). *The organization of behavior: A neuropsychological theory.* Wiley.

Herman, J. L. (1992). *Trauma and recovery: The aftermath of violence—from domestic abuse to political terror.* Basic Books.

Holiday, R. (2014). *The obstacle is the way: The timeless art of turning trials into triumph.* Portfolio/Penguin.

Irvine, W. B. (2009). *A guide to the good life: The ancient art of Stoic joy.* Oxford University Press.

Janet, P. (1889). *Psychological automatism: An essay of experimental psychology on the lower forms of human activity.* Felix Alcan.

Jauk, E., Neubauer, A. C., Toth-Kiraly, I., & Kanske, P. (2017). *The brain of the narcissist: Structural and functional correlates of narcissistic subclinical traits.* Neuroscience & Biobehavioral Reviews, 82, 192–203.

Jung, C. G. (1968). *Man and his symbols.* Dell Publishing.

Keenan-Rieker, M. J., Mims, B. F., Sells, J. N., & O'Gara, E. A. (2018). Spiritual aspects of trauma. In B. F. Mims & J. N. Sells (Eds.), *Counseling troubled students: A guide for practitioners* (pp. 213–236). Springer.

Kirsch, I. (2011). *The social psychology of suggestion and hypnosis. Current Directions in Psychological Science, 20*(4), 226–230.

Leaf, C. (2021). *Cleaning up your mental mess: 5 simple, scientifically proven steps to reduce anxiety, stress, and toxic thinking.* Baker Books.

Levine, P. A. (1997). *Waking the tiger: Healing trauma: The innate capacity to transform overwhelming experiences.* North Atlantic Books.

Linehan, M. M. (1993). *Cognitive-behavioral treatment of borderline personality disorder.* Guilford Press.

Lipton, B. H. (2005). *The biology of belief: Unleashing the power of consciousness, matter & miracles.* Hay House.

Litz, B. T., Stein, N., Delaney, E., Lebowitz, L., Nash, W. P., Silva, C., & Maguen, S. (2009). *Moral injury and moral repair in war veterans: A preliminary conceptual framework and treatment implications.* Clinical Psychology Review, 29(7), 695–706.

Lupker, S. J., Pardoel, A., & O'Bryan, P. (2020). *When and why does articulation influence task switching?* Journal of Experimental Psychology: Learning, Memory, and Cognition, 46(5), 978–995.

Maslow, A. H. (1943). *A theory of human motivation.* Psychological Review, 50(4), 370–396.

Maslow, A. H. (1968). *Toward a psychology of being* (2nd ed.). D. Van Nostrand Company.

Mauss, I. B., Tamir, M., Anderson, C. L., & Savino, N. S. (2011). *Can seeking happiness make people unhappy? Paradoxical effects of valuing happiness. Emotion*, 11(4), 807–815.

McEwen, B. S., & Sapolsky, R. M. (1995). *Stress and cognitive function. Current Opinion in Neurobiology*, *5*(2), 205–216.

McLynn, F. (2009). *Marcus Aurelius: A life.* Da Capo Press.

Mineka, S., Watson, D., & Clark, L. A. (1998). *Comorbidity of anxiety and unipolar mood disorders.* Annual Review of Psychology, *49*(1), 377–411.

Mittal, V., Kim, S. E., Chen, S., & Northoff, G. (2020). *The spontaneous thought episode: A theory of the functional neuroanatomy of resting-state cognition.* Neuroscience & Biobehavioral Reviews, 118, 644–653.

Nardo, D. D., Wachen, J. S., Boffa, J. W., & Nardo, C. M. (2018). *The Reconsolidation of Traumatic Memories (RTM) protocol for PTSD: A case study.* Journal of Loss and Trauma, 23(8), 698–708.

Neff, K. D. (2003). *Self-compassion: An alternative conceptualization of a healthy attitude toward oneself.* Self and Identity, *2*(2), 85–101.

Nickerson, R. S. (1998). *Confirmation bias: A ubiquitous phenomenon in many guises.* Review of General Psychology, 2(2), 175–220.

Ní Dhúill, C., Zabel, J., & Liddle, P. F. (2019). *The effects of ketamine on resting-state oscillatory power and connectivity.* NeuroImage, *203*, 116172.

Nolen-Hoeksema, S. (1998). *The role of rumination in depressive disorders and mixed anxiety/depressive symptoms.* Journal of Abnormal Psychology, 107(3), 561

Peterson, C., & Seligman, M. E. P. (2004). *Character strengths and virtues: A handbook and classification.* American Psychological Association; Oxford University Press.

Plutchik, R. (1980). *Emotion: A psychoevolutionary synthesis.* Harper & Row.

Porges, S. W. (2011). *The polyvagal theory: Neurophysiological foundations of emotions, attachment, communication, and self-regulation.* W. W. Norton & Company.

Real, T. (2022). *Us: Getting past you and me to build a more loving relationship.* Goop Press; Rodale Books.

Rahula, W. (1974). *What the Buddha taught.* Grove Press.

Robbins, M. (2024). *The "Let Them" theory: Courage to choose yourself.* Simon & Schuster.

Robson, D. (2022). *The expectation effect: How your mind can transform your life.* Henry Holt and Co.

Rotter, J. B. (1966). *Generalized expectancies for internal versus external control of reinforcement.* Psychological Monographs: General and Applied, 80(1), 1–28.

Sherman, L. E., Payton, A. A., Hernandez, L. M., Greenfield, P. M., & Dapretto, M. (2016). *The power of the like in adolescence: Effects of peer endorsement on neural activity.* Psychological Science, 27(7), 1027–1035.

Teresa, M. (1996). *The joy in loving: A guide to daily living* (J. Chaliha & E. Le Joly, Comps.). Viking.

van der Hart, O., Nijenhuis, E. R. S., & Steele, K. (2006). *The haunted self: Structural dissociation and the treatment of chronic traumatization*. W. W. Norton & Company.

van der Kolk, B. A. (2014). *The body keeps the score: Brain, mind, and body in the healing of trauma*. Penguin Books.

VanderWeele, T. J., Wortham, J. M., Carey, M. B., Case, B. W., Cowden, R. G., Duffee, C., Jackson-Meyer, K., Lu, F., Mattson, S. A., & Padgett, R. N. (2025). *Moral trauma, moral distress, moral injury, and moral injury disorder: Definitions and assessments*. Frontiers in Psychology, 16, Article 1422441.

Vignola, N. (2024). *Rewire: Break the Cycle, Alter Your Thoughts and Create Lasting Change*. HarperOne.

Watts, A. (1975). *Tao: The watercourse way*. Pantheon Books.

ABOUT THE AUTHOR

DANIEL SUNDAHL (AKA DANSUN) is a counselling therapist, internationally recognized artist, and keynote speaker dedicated to raising awareness around trauma and mental health. Daniel spent two decades on the front lines of emergency services, witnessing firsthand the visceral realities of extreme stress as an advanced care paramedic and career firefighter. It was these experiences that sparked his mission to bridge the gap between high-stress environments and clinical recovery.

Daniel's work is a rare synthesis of a life lived at the extremes; his journey as a world traveller gave him a global perspective on human resilience, while his years as a first responder provided a visceral understanding of the front lines of trauma and the human experience. As an artist, he developed the precision to capture the raw, emotional truths of those experiences. As a clinician and author, he has combined that insight into a clear and welcoming way to help and connect with others. This unique intersection of high-stakes experience and clinical expertise allows him to blend technical neurobiology with deep, artistic storytelling that validates and supports those he works with.

Born in Edmonton, Alberta, Canada, Daniel's perspective is shaped by a truly global background, having lived and taught in the Cayman Islands, Egypt, Mexico, Indonesia, and Japan. This international journey has allowed him to collaborate with peers in Australia,

Finland, the United Kingdom, Guatemala, Poland, and the United States, providing him with a unique, cross-cultural understanding of resilience. Daniel now works full-time as a counselor, artist, author, and public speaker, travelling the world to help individuals build a permanent foundation of peace by overcoming old, fear-based pathways.

www.ingramcontent.com/pod-product-compliance
Ingram Content Group UK Ltd.
Pitfield, Milton Keynes, MK11 3LW, UK
UKHW022002190726
13853UKWH00004B/1687